St. Madeleine Sophie Barat

St. Madeleine Sophie Barat

Leadership in a Divided World

Juliet Mousseau, RSCJ

Paulist Press
New York / Mahwah, NJ

Photo/Image Credits: Courtesy of the Society of the Sacred Heart Archives, United States-Canada Province

Cover image: Icon of Philippine Duchesne and Sophie Barat by Anne Davidson, RSCJ
Cover and book design by Lynn Else

Library of Congress Cataloging-in-Publication Data
Names: Mousseau, Juliet, author.
Title: St. Madeleine Sophie Barat: leadership in a divided world / Juliet Mousseau, RSCJ.
Description: New York: Paulist Press, [2025] | Summary: "This biography tells the story of Madeleine Sophie Barat, a Frenchwoman who in the middle of the violence of the French Revolution founded the Society of the Sacred Heart, a religious institution that now has schools around the world"—Provided by publisher.
Identifiers: LCCN 2024036559 (print) | LCCN 2024036560 (ebook) | ISBN 9780809157495 (paperback) | ISBN 9780809189168 (ebook)
Subjects: LCSH: Barat, Madeleine-Sophie, Saint, 1779–1865. | Nuns—France—Biography. | Christian women saints—France—Biography.
Classification: LCC BX4700.M2 M68 2025 (print) | LCC BX4700.M2 (ebook) | DDC 271/.97 [B]—dc23/eng/20250110
LC record available at https://lccn.loc.gov/2024036559
LC ebook record available at https://lccn.loc.gov/2024036560

ISBN 978-0-8091-5749-5 (paperback)
ISBN 978-0-8091-8916-8 (ebook)

Published by Paulist Press
997 Macarthur Boulevard
Mahwah, NJ 07430
www.paulistpress.com

Printed and bound in the
United States of America

To Sophie and her companions, past, present,
and for generations to come

Contents

Contents

List of Illustrations

Foreword

JULIET MOUSSEAU'S presentation of the life of Madeleine Sophie Barat is a joy to read. Mousseau offers us a clear, nuanced perspective on Sophie's journey, drawing from the monumental research of Phil Kilroy[1] while also choosing judiciously from other sources. In so doing, she brings to life key dimensions of Sophie's growth as a Religious of the Sacred Heart and as the founder and leader of the congregation. Responding to the invitation that Barbara Dawson, superior general of the Society of the Sacred Heart, made to a new generation of RSCJ scholars, Mousseau contributes the richness of her academic background to exploring various aspects of the Society's life and mission.

I have often thought that to understand Sophie's life, challenges, and choices, one needed to understand the history of Europe in her time, particularly the developments in France and neighboring countries, the dynamics within the Church, and the interrelationship of ecclesial affairs with those of the various nation-states. As one whose only study of European history was in the tenth grade, I have a long learning curve! Mousseau describes, highlights, and contextualizes the influences that shaped significant moments in Sophie's journey in a way that I found both clarifying and enlightening.

This biography shows us Sophie's growing understanding of the essential elements of the charism of the congregation she was called to lead. She had a strong sense of God's desire to make known the love of the Heart of Jesus through an education that embodied this love. Furthermore, Sophie wished to contribute to the rebuilding of the fabric of French society following the revolution. She also had intuitions and convictions about the style, shape, and structures that would be needed for a unified, international congregation. Yet she often did not see the way forward and was "learning on the job"—being attentive to the depth and direction of the call in her own life, listening to the Spirit as the call took root in the lives of her sisters, sensing the essential elements of that call, and designing ways to ground the lives of her future sisters in that call.

Mousseau gives us insight into Sophie's own growth in her vocation, her personal struggle to believe in the love of God she could describe so well to others, and her challenges in giving direction to "this little Society" when others wanted to exercise influence or control. As we read her life in our own time of epochal change and transformation, Sophie's journey calls us—Religious of the Sacred Heart, Associates, and partners in mission—to continually plumb the depths of the charism in our own relationship with God and the ways we live Jesus's love. We seek to ensure that this charism is at the core of new developments, expanded perceptions of mission, and recontextualized articulations of the vision that are ours to live in the twenty-first century.

Similarly, at a time when many in our world are shaping new structures for organization and governance in civil society, projects, and religious congregations, Sophie has solid experience to offer us. Her clear focus on mission and purpose guided her choices. It is often said that she governed through relationships. Mousseau shows how Sophie's contemplation of the heart of Jesus where she experienced love that was personal, tender, caring, and strong led her to act in that same way with others. Sophie's preferred style of governance was through influence rather than from authority. Her personal approach, coming to know the interiority of a person and letting herself be known, surely helped her sisters to grow in prayer, in the generosity of their commitment, and in the grounded, flexible, and creative ways they adapted to new situations. This personal focus also helped to create union among those who were geographically dispersed. The ambiguities of governing by relationship—which were also evident—called her to reflect on and live her capacity for relationship in a deeper context, with the courage to keep the clarity of the mission to which she was called in the forefront of her choices. The challenges we meet today are different, but we, too, are invited to live this integration of relationship and mission in our own times.

I also appreciated the glimpses into the developments of the Society on the American frontier. Sophie and Philippine Duchesne were soul friends from the early days of the Society, each with dreams of far-reaching mission. Their life journeys were drawn from the same source while the cultural, socioeconomic, and political contexts in which they lived this out could hardly have been more different. Their desire and experience of maintaining union in such diversity can give us courage and inspiration today as the Society and the Church evolve into new meanings of living the gospel within the complexity of cultures, values, politics, and socioeconomic realities of our world.

Throughout this book, brief comments on Sophie's health, usually when Sophie was suffering from illness or falls or simply exhaustion, chronicle her challenges in living the physical dimensions of her life. This can offer us encouragement. We see in Sophie a woman who accepts her limitations (not always easily!) and finds creative ways to use her times of illness for prayer, correspondence, or deeper reflection. Then, living *with* the limitations of her health, she continues her journeys, for the mission she feels called to also renews her energy. *Caritas Christi urget nos!* (2 Cor 5:14). May we in times of fragility or diminishment draw inspiration and courage to find new paths for living the mission of love.

Mousseau's biography of Sophie is an accessible resource for those sharing the life and mission of the Society today and for anyone searching for how to live gospel values in the complexities of our era. Those familiar with Sophie may find new clarity or perspective, and those coming to know her will find this a wonderful opportunity to delve into her story. May Sophie draw us to open ourselves more deeply to God's love and confirm in us the courage to bring that love flowing from an open and pierced heart to our own contexts.

Kathleen Conan, RSCJ
Superior General, 2008–2016
Society of the Sacred Heart of Jesus

Acknowledgments

MY FIRST introduction to Sophie came during the novitiate, when I read and reread Phil Kilroy's historical biography and Margaret Williams's more hagiographical account of Sophie's life. I am grateful to both of these Religious of the Sacred Heart for showing me Sophie's personality and liveliness, which drew me closer to her.

In exploring Sophie's life and context as a historian and writer, I am grateful for the incredible historical and archival work of Phil Kilroy, which lies at the core of this biography. Likewise, I am grateful that at her retirement our superior general, Sister Barbara Dawson, entrusted to me and others the task of carrying on Phil's work for our own generation and world. I am both delighted and daunted by the task and its significance for today.

Sophie left us abundant resources, as one might expect from sixty-five years of service as mother general. Of her letters, fourteen thousand have been collected by the General Archives of the Society of the Sacred Heart in Rome. The process of scanning and transcribing them is underway, and some translations and partial translations are available. The work of the archivists, including Margaret Phelan, RSCJ, former archivist, and a group of many sisters and lay collaborators move this enormous project forward. I am grateful for the assistance of Federica Palumbo, General Archivist, Alice Usai, and Sara

Giannetti in providing materials from the General Archives in Rome.

I am also grateful to Sisters Lyn Osiek, Fran Gimber, Kathleen Hughes, and Mary Charlotte Chandler for encouraging me to develop my understanding of Sophie and her times. A special thank you to Lyn and Fran for spotting any factual errors. Any that remain are entirely my own.

I extend my gratitude to the countless RSCJ and other members of the Sacred Heart family who have encouraged me to complete this project. May the beauty and love of Sophie's life continue to inspire new generations.

Introduction: A Humble Heart

Learn from me, for I am meek
and humble of heart.

Matthew 11:29 in Constitutions (1815), 72

SOPHIE BARAT'S life reads like an eighty-five-year-long lesson in gentleness and humility. The trials she faced while bringing the Society of the Sacred Heart into existence were met with courage and prayer. She united herself with the heart of Jesus in contemplation and gathered strength from Christ himself. Her leadership, her focus on personal relationships, and her patience amid adversity allowed her to navigate a polarized world while retaining her personal integrity.

From childhood, Sophie's spunk and generosity drew people to her. Stories from every stage of her life highlight her close friendships and loyalty to family and friends. The fourteen thousand letters that are held in the Sacred Heart archives testify to her capacity for intimate conversation even when she was far from those she loved. As the superior of the Society of the Sacred Heart from 1800 to 1865, she guided sisters by seeing into their hearts and speaking to their deepest needs, either in person or by letter. Her letters also reveal gentle yet firm communication to achieve the desired outcome while strengthening personal relationships even among people with whom she disagreed.

The context of her life brought Sophie to envision a new way of being a woman religious. The French Revolution emerged from social unrest and economic injustice, bringing violence that traumatized an entire country. Society was divided, government was upended, and what had been certain could no longer be relied on. The Catholic Church, because it was identified as part of the noble classes, was distrusted, and Catholics found themselves in great danger. Members of religious orders and priests were killed by the guillotine along with others considered traitors. And yet, Sophie felt within her a call seeking to live in the convent. As her call developed, she discovered that the world needed her gifts and those of others like her to help rebuild the structures and norms of society that were lost in the chaos of war and political upheaval.

But the world had changed in her still-short lifetime, and a new form of religious life was needed. Sophie envisioned a life in which solid contemplative prayer provided the spiritual support one needed to testify to God's love in the chaos of the secular world. The model of religious life for women, separated from the world by walls and grilles, safe from secular influence, would not enable the type of direct impact on society that she envisioned.

In her quest to realize her new vision of religious life, Sophie found both helpful and destructive forces, and yet figures on both sides wanted her to conform to the traditional ways of working. Her gentle (and genteel) manner of approaching authoritative figures with humility slowly wore away their resistance and brought them to see the value of her vision. Her best mentors learned to trust her leadership style and helped her move forward, while her worst detractors found themselves on the wrong side of history. She found partners to join her campaign of God's love, and her long term of leadership placed the Society of the Sacred Heart on a solid foundation.

Sophie's story reveals a holy woman who was also wholly human. Her patience with difficult situations and people, her capacity to hear what others advised and then to act as she knew was right, and her strength of character to stand up to men (and a few women) who tried to bully her into backing down—these characteristics make her a saint for today's church and world. Above all, she viewed everything through the lens of the heart of Jesus, responding in loving compassion to everyone she encountered, and inspiring others to follow her in doing the same.

1

From Fire to Revolution

THE DARK NIGHT of December 12, 1779, was interrupted with fire—not fire that brought good food and warm homes, but fire that had the potential to tear through a town and cause destruction and death. Fortunately, this fire caused minimal damage. However, the distress it caused brought a bundle of joy: Madame Barat went into labor two months prematurely, and a tiny girl was born at 11:00 p.m. whom her parents named Madeleine Sophie Barat. Afraid she would not live through the communal trauma of her birth, she was whisked to the church and baptized immediately, her older brother and a neighbor serving as impromptu godparents. So tiny and precious, Sophie was already marked by both trauma and great love.

The precarious nature of her mother's early labor gave way to a childhood filled with wonder in the small vineyard community of Joigny, France. The medieval town sat along the Yonne River, extending up the gentle slopes of the hills, where the community vines—covering around 550 hectares—took over the land. Young Sophie would run among them when she was freed from her school and household tasks. Monsieur Jacques Barat made barrels for the wine produced in the area, and Madame Madeleine Fouffé, Sophie's mother, cared for the three children of the household. Louis and Marie-Louise were eleven and ten years old when Sophie made her dramatic entrance into the family. The events of her birth would become legendary, as the young Sophie, when asked "What brought you into the world?" would answer "It was fire." She became known as the "child of fire," which also reflected her determined nature and warm, loving personality.

Sophie's older brother had a profound influence on Sophie's life. Louis Barat left home when Sophie was a small child, entering the seminary at Sens to study for the priesthood. Louis's education was typical for a man preparing to minister in the church. By the time he completed his courses, he was not yet old enough to be ordained to the priesthood, so he returned home to Joigny to teach in the local school and continue his studies. Sophie, eight years old, was entrusted to him for her education, a task he took seriously. Curious, intelligent, and ready for a teacher, she received from him the same curriculum he gave to the boys in the school. Alongside the excellent education he offered, Sophie also received the harsh nature of his asceticism, which would shape her character and theology throughout her life.

The spiritual world of Louis and Sophie was marked by Jansenism, a pessimistic worldview that focused on the sinfulness of human nature. The teachings of Cornelius Jansen (1585–1638) took hold in France following the posthumous publication of his biography of St. Augustine. In *Augustinus*, Jansen wrestled with the relationship between grace and free will. He believed that the Counter Reformation movements placed too much emphasis on the goodness of humanity and discounted the profound effect of sin on human nature. Thus, Jansenism focused on the damage caused by original sin and the need for the utter reliance on God's grace. This theological movement shaped spirituality in France in the seventeenth and eighteenth centuries, and it also became attached to the political events around the French Revolution. Pope Innocent V condemned five propositions of Jansenism in 1653, leading to a division among French clergy. Pope Clement XI again condemned Jansenism in both 1705 and 1713. The final condemnation became French law in 1730. Though this marked the official end of Jansenism as a faction of the church in France, ideas held among Jansenists and a generally negative view of humanity continued to affect mainstream Catholic thought for many generations. Jesuits led the charge in opposing these ideas, focusing instead on the capacity of the human person for good and the role of free will in response to God's grace, and encouraging frequent confession and communion.

Jansenism was swept up in the greater political divisions within France and between the French church and Rome. The pope and his rejection of Jansenism aligned with the French monarchy, while Jansenism was identified with the interests of the French *parlement*. In this case, alignment with the monarchy also meant being placed in the Ultramontane camp, those who allowed for Rome to have some authority over the Catholic Church in France. When the revolutionaries with Gallican ideas (those who opposed the Ultramontane view) held power in France, public display of the image of the Sacred Heart put Catholics in danger. Because the image of the Sacred Heart of Jesus implied a loving and generous God, in contradiction to the Jansenist message of sin and depravity, it, too, became aligned with politics. When Louis Barat sent home an image of the Sacred Hearts of Jesus and Mary, his mother, devoted to her seminarian son, affixed it to the wall in the family home. She probably did not know of its political significance.

The influence of Jansenism can be seen in Louis Barat's harsh understanding of human nature. He was vigilant over

Sophie's education and behavior, particularly requiring penances of her throughout her life. Geneviève Deshayes, later a companion of Sophie, said of Louis's care for Sophie that he

> was more concerned about the spiritual development of his sister than experienced in the physical care such a fragile and delicate child needed....He dreamed of making her a saint and for this reason did not neglect her education....He made her work without the breaks necessary for her age and suited to her physical strength. She was truly imprisoned; maybe if she had been less held she would have gained less too; but her body always suffered from the effect of this handling in childhood.[1]

Little is known about the influence of Sophie's sister Marie-Louise on her childhood. Sophie was a teenager when Marie-Louise married in 1793. Sophie served as godmother to her children, and she remained loyal to Marie-Louise and the children throughout her life.

The upheaval of revolution also shaped Sophie's early life. The French Revolution began with the Estates General of 1789, convoked in response to widespread social unrest and economic depression. The years between 1789 and 1799 were exceptionally violent. Governmental structures in Joigny changed through a vote, and political demonstrations were common even there, so far from the capital. The new government affected the church as well, as most priests were members of the nobility. Afraid that a foreign government might try to influence the church in France, *parlement* demanded that a new French church be established without recognition from the papacy. Priests were required to sign an oath of fidelity to the French church by 1791, and those who did not were to be punished severely. The government suppressed religious orders in 1790, and many religious were imprisoned or sent home. Louis, who had already been ordained a deacon, at first made the oath, and then retracted it after learning that the pope condemned those who took it. He was imprisoned for two-and-a-half years and narrowly escaped the guillotine. His family, too, were endangered by his recantation, and the local government put them under surveillance and sequestered their goods. When Louis was released in 1795, he went into hiding, ministering to Catholics in secret. The family's troubles only ended when they could convince the authorities that they were not members of the noble class.

Louis's imprisonment led Madame Barat into a time of mental imbalance, depression, and anxiety. Sophie, still only twelve or thirteen, cared for her mother and nursed her back to health. Sophie prodded her mother to eat, making her favorite foods and refusing to eat until she did. Though young, she also took on the administrative tasks of running the household, allowing her mother the time and space she needed to recover from her illness. The love and compassion required to respond to the situation in this way would influence Sophie's personality later in life. She continued to check in on her mother and her sister throughout her lifetime, eventually also guiding her nieces and nephews as they grew into adulthood. Loyalty and fidelity to family was never lost, despite the hardships she faced with Louis as she came of age.

The time of Louis's imprisonment also cemented the role of the Sacred Heart of Jesus in Sophie's spirituality. Pictures of the Sacred Heart of Jesus and the Immaculate Heart of Mary, sent by Louis and hung in the family home, were the center of the family's prayer. Sophie later remarked that this was her introduction to the Sacred Heart of Jesus.[2] The complexities of the French government in revolution and the spiritual shift happening in the French church point to the multiplicity of influences on Sophie's early life. Revolution caused chaos and a loss of moral order in the society, ills that Sophie believed could be mitigated through proper education. Later in life, she would focus her attention on the often-overlooked educational needs of young women of the middle and upper classes. Sophie saw the disruption caused by social upheaval, and she believed that women of some means could have a powerful humanizing effect in society by influencing their husbands and children. These male family members were active in the public sphere, directing the new phase the nation of France was entering. Strong women, well educated in the ways of the world and in their faith and morals, would shape their husbands' beliefs and educate their children in the proper ways to contribute to society. Thus, the gift of education went beyond the child receiving it to have a multigenerational impact on France and the society as a whole.

Image 1: Portrait of Sophie as a young girl, which hangs in her family home in Joigny, France.

Sophie left Joigny in 1795 at the age of fifteen to go to Paris with Louis, who had recently been ordained to the priesthood. Sophie believed that his guidance was God's will for her, and she went with him to continue her education under his tutelage. Whether Sophie felt a call to religious life by that point is unclear, but it remained impossible as religious orders continued to be suppressed. Sophie and Louis moved into a house where his identity would be kept secret, owned by Madame Duval. Together with three companions, Marguerite (Madame Duval's maid, whose last name was not recorded), Octavie Bailly, and Marie-Françoise Loquet, Sophie followed the order of day established by Louis, which was modeled on the Trappist monastery. Centering their life on prayer and study, they attended daily Mass, kept silence and cloister, and had little food or sleep. The women studied scripture, Latin, mathematics, and the church fathers. Some time was left for needlework, but Louis burned or gave away anything Sophie created for him or herself. The austerity of his order of life and the harsh nature of his interactions with her, though they were guided by his care for her spirit, had a detrimental effect on her physical body. He controlled her whole life, determining what she could eat, do, and study, and forbidding her to leave the house for any but the most serious reason. Sophie obeyed without question and took her suffering as a form of sacrifice to God.

While in Paris, Louis gave Sophie an education that mirrored his own studies. Both Barat siblings were bright and eager learners, and Louis recognized the potential of his little sister. They remained in Paris until 1797 when it became too dangerous for Louis and then returned to Joigny for a time. Sophie, changed by the treatment of her brother, declared her desire to enter the Carmelites, which continued to be impossible. Louis returned to Paris in 1799, and Sophie followed soon after.

2

Community Beginnings

SOPHIE'S DESIRE for a life of contemplation among the Carmelites, nurtured by her early education under Louis, was now to be shaped by the people around her and the needs of the community. Sophie was one of many women and men of the nineteenth century who sought to undo the chaos of the French Revolution by dedicating their lives to address the religious and societal needs of the time. In 1799, she encountered Fr. Joseph Varin, who became one of her supporters and guides. Fr. Varin was among the many priests working to reestablish the Jesuits, who had been suppressed in Europe in 1774. He also supported different religious orders along the way, promoting the vision of Fr. Léonor de Tournély (d. 1797), who established a group of religious priests called the Society of the Sacred Heart. Fr. de Tournély wanted to form a religious community of women under the same name, and Fr. Varin took up his cause.

A priest named Fr. Niccolo Paccanari was the founder of an Italian group of men called the Fathers of the Sacred Heart. When the two groups met, they decided to merge, and they became known as the Fathers of the Faith. Fr. Varin introduced Fr. Paccanari to a group of women he knew who wished to support the reinstatement of the Jesuits. Fr. Paccanari, too, had envisioned an order of women, and he had established a rule for a group called the Dilette di Gesù, the Beloved of Jesus. The rule he wrote incorporated a fully active life through education with a fully contemplative life that sought to make amends for the sins of the world. Their double focus represented the expectation that women religious would remain cloistered.

With the union of the French and Italian Fathers of the Faith, Fr. Varin was entrusted to promote both the Fathers of the Faith and the Dilette di Gesù in France after the Revolution. He encouraged Sophie to rethink her decision to enter the Carmelites and instead join the Dilette di Gesù. In fact, he informed her that it was God's will for her. She accepted Fr. Varin's suggestion. Her three companions in Paris, Marguerite, Octavie, and Marie-Françoise, were also longing for religious life, and they joined Sophie to become a new house of the Dilette. Because she was a more prominent figure in Paris as the author of several well-known novels, Fr. Varin believed Marie-Françoise Loquet would be best suited to leadership and assigned her to be superior of the little group. In this new group of religious women, Fr. Varin brought to life the charism and foundation both of the Dilette and of Fr. de Tournély's vision for a companion order to the Jesuits.

The four companions celebrated their affiliation with the Dilette on November 21, 1800, following some days of retreat. Sophie recalled the event later:

> As I had never seen a religious ceremony, this one, simple as it was, made a profound impression on me. When we left the chapel we placed before the altar a candle that was to burn till evening in sign of thanksgiving. At dinner time Father Varin, my brother and Father Roger were at table with us; it was like the *agape* of the first Christians, full of

> sweet and religious expansiveness. The meal was prolonged beyond our usual time and we were still there when a friend of ours came to call. Not wishing to disturb us she went first to the chapel, and what was her fright on seeing that the altar cloth was on fire! She gave the alarm and the danger was checked; in a few moments the whole altar would have been in a blaze and perhaps the house would have burned down, who knows? It is thus that the demon began to make war on us at our very birth, and the divine Master to protect us.[1]

Fire once again marked a significant moment in Sophie's life.

While promoting the expansion of the Fathers of the Faith in France, Fr. Varin continued to support the growth of the Dilette. During a visit to Amiens in 1801, he encountered a group of three women running a small boarding school that was becoming too much for them to run alone. Fr. Varin introduced the women from Paris to this small group, envisioning that they could work together in the school in Amiens. Two of them, Genevieve Deshayes and Henriette Grosier, affiliated with the Dilette, and the school became the first house of the new religious order. Marie-Françoise Loquet remained the superior over the growing community. Sophie and Octavie soon joined her and the others in Amiens. Octavie was sent to Rome to be trained as a mistress of novices.

Sophie, Geneviève, and Henriette took on the teaching duties of the school while Marie-Françoise led the group as superior of the house. The three teachers were new to the task, learning both how to teach and how to live as religious at the same time. Sophie struggled a great deal, sometimes seeming disconnected from the world around her. She also experienced repeated illnesses. Loquet was not the competent leader that Varin expected her to be, instead causing chaos through her inattention to the needs of the sisters. It was a very austere time for the community.

Fr. Varin continued to be in close contact with the community, though he remained unaware of the problems caused by Loquet's inability to serve as superior. In 1802 he found three more women who had heard of the Dilette and wished to join the community. Later that year, in December 1802, the superior general of the Dilette from Rome, Louise Naudet, visited Amiens. She stayed for several months, and in that time, she persuaded Marie-Françoise Loquet that religious life was not her calling. Before she left, she named Sophie, just twenty-three, as the next superior.

Image 2. The first house of the Society of the Sacred Heart in Amiens.

Though the house experienced relief at the departure of Marie-Françoise, Sophie inherited the problems she had created. In her new role as superior, she relied on the guidance of Louise Naudet and Fr. Niccolo Paccanari, both in Rome. Fr. Varin, though also supportive, required all her decisions to pass through him before being implemented. He also assigned two local priests to be advisors to Sophie and confessors to the school and community, Fr. Bruson and Fr. Sambucy de Saint-Estève. Anne Baudemont was named assistant to Sophie, and Geneviève Deshayes was placed in charge of the studies at the school.

Sophie found the task of leadership oppressive, and her health suffered so much that she came close to death. After much encouragement, she received treatment in Paris lasting several months until she was able to resume the role of community superior. The community continued to grow, as did political tensions. Napoleon's rule over France heightened tensions with Rome, and the new religious order under Sophie had to separate from the Italian Dilette. Additionally, it was revealed that Fr. Paccanari was both a controversial and a criminal figure, and the French Fathers of the Faith likewise severed their ties with the Roman group. This separation caused Sophie to lose the support she had from Louise Naudet. In the course of all this, Octavie returned from training in Rome and decided to leave the community. She became a Carmelite, another loss for Sophie. The community rechristened themselves the Association des Dames de l'Instruction Chrétienne. Though these separations were difficult for Sophie, the distance from the two established orders allowed her to express her own vision of religious life. She explained her impulse late in her life:

> The first idea of the Society that we had...was to gather as many as possible of the true adorers of the Heart of Jesus in the Eucharist....At the end of the Terror and of the abominations of the Revolution against religion and the Blessed Sacrament... all hearts vibrated together in unison: Make reparations to Jesus Christ in the Blessed Sacrament... was the rallying cry....No two pious people meeting

> together would talk without trying to find some means of bringing Jesus Christ back into family life.
>
> My original idea of our little Society of the Sacred Heart was to gather young girls together and establish *a little community which night and day would adore the Heart of Jesus, whose love had been desecrated in the Eucharist.* But I said to myself, when we are twenty-four religious, able to replace one another on a prie-dieu for perpetual adoration, that will be something, and yet little enough for such a noble goal....If we had *young pupils* whom we formed in the spirit of adoration and reparation, now that would be different! and I saw hundreds, thousands of adorers before a *perfect, universal monstrance, raised above the Church.*
>
> "That is it" I said to myself, as I was praying before a lonely tabernacle: "we must dedicate ourselves to the education of youth, renew in souls the foundations of a living faith in the...Blessed Sacrament; [and] there fight the traces of Jansenism which had led to [such] impiety. With the revelations of Jesus Christ to Blessed Margaret Mary concerning the devotion of reparation...to the Heart of Jesus in the Blessed Sacrament, we will raise up a multitude of adorers from all the nations, to the very ends of the earth."[2]

The passion and joy expressed in this vision would inspire the women who joined Sophie, but it would take decades to come to fulfillment in the Society of the Sacred Heart. It seemed inevitable that a movement arising from the chaos of revolutionary France would face tumultuous beginnings and growth.

3

Philippine Duchesne

WHILE SOPHIE was establishing the first community in Paris and then joining with the community in Amiens, other developments were taking place in Grenoble that soon become part of the story of the Society of the Sacred Heart. These events involve Rose Philippine Duchesne.

Philippine Duchesne was born in Grenoble in 1769. She grew up with her eight siblings and an extended family of many cousins. She was educated at home by a governess with her cousins until it was time to receive first communion. At that time, as was the custom, she was sent to the local Visitation convent, Sainte Marie d'en Haut, to continue her studies in 1781. While there, Philippine felt the desire to enter religious life. When her parents learned this, they brought her home in 1784, hoping to dissuade her. When her cousin married in 1788, Philippine went to the convent and refused to return home. Her parents relented on the condition that she would not profess vows until she reached twenty-five years of age.

The political situation in France interfered. Philippine had to leave Sainte Marie d'en Haut in 1792 when all convents and monasteries in France were suppressed. She returned home and continued to live as a nun to the best of her ability. When the fiercest of the persecutions ended in 1795, the Visitation communities around the country began to regroup. Philippine wanted the same to happen in Grenoble, and so she began to work toward that goal. Her cousins helped her regain access to the convent, which had been claimed by the French government during the Revolution. Then, from 1801 to 1804 she strove to bring together the Visitation sisters who had lived there before. She gathered companions and set up life there—an austere life that reflected the austerity of the dilapidated building—but it proved to be too great an undertaking.

Once she realized she was unable to restore the community as it had been before the Revolution, Philippine began searching for others to join or support her or a community for her to join. She heard about the work of the Fathers of the Faith and of the Dilette in Italy, and Fr. Varin came to visit her. Seeing Philippine's passion and the work she had done, he determined the community at Sainte Marie d'en Haut would be an appropriate addition to Sophie's fledgling religious order. He sent Sophie to Grenoble in 1804 to meet Philippine.

Sophie arrived in Grenoble on December 13, 1804, with two sisters from Amiens. The encounter of the two communities was exciting, hopeful, and tense. Sophie was weak from illness and still lacked confidence in her leadership role. The others found her serious and withdrawn, and many avoided her. Sophie decided to start the novitiate of the new community after Christmas, beginning with a retreat. The retreat was led by Fr. Pierre Roger, and it turned into a fiasco. Fr. Roger had little experience, and the group soon discovered his methodology was unhelpful. "Finally, on the last day of the retreat the entire group, including Roger, fell about laughing in the little prayer room. Such an experience helped more than anything else to break down barriers of shyness and reserve between the women, and to bond them together."[1]

Sophie led the subsequent novitiate training. There is little known about the content of the formation program, but Sophie made it clear that the new community was no longer the Visitation. First, she removed the grilles that were a traditional part of cloistered monastic life. In doing so, Sophie indicated a new relationship with outsiders, a closer connection that allowed for more natural human interaction. Philippine struggled greatly with this decision, as it marked for her a break with tradition. The second change Sophie wished to make was to stop reciting the Office in choir, replacing it with an extended period of silent prayer. This, a practice of the Dilette, would allow the sisters to rest their voices after teaching all day. However, the suggestion caused an uproar in the wider Grenoble community, who wanted them to continue praying as the Visitation convent had prayed. While this change was soon reversed, it illustrated Sophie's desire to adapt the monastic lifestyle to one more suited to active life.

Image 3. Ste-Marie-d'en-Haut, the Visitation Monastery in Grenoble.

The novitiate schedule was modeled on the pattern of life at Amiens. In late 1805, Frs. Varin and Roger adapted the Rule of the Dilette for this community, and it was approved as a provisional rule by the local bishop. The five novices made their first profession to this rule on November 21, 1805.

This initial formation for Philippine and the Grenoble companions would lead to Philippine's call to share the Sacred Heart with the people of the New World. In 1806, Sophie wrote to her at length of her vision and hopes for this missionary activity:

> Even before I knew our little Society, the desire of bringing the name of our Lord to non-Christian people was deep in my heart. It grew stronger as I got to know the Jesuit missionaries, and St. Francis Xavier became my patron. Several graces that I obtained through his intercession made me hope that my prayers had been heard and that he would take me to these people steeped in darkness. One day, urged more than usual by this strong desire, I spoke about it to a kindred soul. I thought that this holy man would give me the sort of answer that I was hoping for. But what an answer! Quickly I banished from my mind the idea that here was a prophet, and said inwardly: "Surely he must be mistaken!" "No, no," he said after a few moments of thought, "France is your mission field; you will not leave it."
>
> I went away sad, but tried to resign myself to the fact, if it must be. Time has shown him to be right, and that I must abandon this desire. Now God's manifest will in my election has snatched away any vestige of hope that might have remained. I am tied to France and to its neighbouring countries. Does this mean I have given up the idea? No,

> the desire is growing daily, and I ask that one of my companions may carry it out, that the Holy Spirit Himself will guide her. If in our lifetime we cannot go so far afield, may there be souls of prayer, zealous for the salvation of these people, who will pass on their zeal to others who, in God's good time, when His wisdom and goodness see fit, will be ready to go to distant lands.
>
> I can see you pleading at the feet of our Lord, asking if it is you whom He calls to this work. Don't expect me to give an answer just yet; but hope, stimulate the desires you have, and strive to make yourself worthy of this outstanding grace. Let us both pray especially for this. How happy I should be if our Lord, since He has so many reasons for refusing my offers to help, would accept yours! Whilst we are awaiting this happy day, striving to hasten it by the purity of our lives and the fervour of our prayers, I want you to know that perhaps one door will be opened soon; our Lord and I are very busy about this—just as He has inspired you with the same ideas.[2]

It would be many years before Sophie could send Philippine into the wilderness of North America. We can see in their intimate sharing the seeds of a strong friendship and common goal—to share God's love with those who do not know it. Sophie shows her growing confidence as a relational leader, building up communities by spending time with them and getting to know her sisters. She discovered Philippine's "heart of oak" (the meaning of "Duchesne") in her hard work reestablishing the Grenoble convent and her courageous dream of ministering among the Native Americans in an unknown land. These two women's shared dream and contrasting personalities formed the core of the Society of the Sacred Heart as it came into existence.

4

The First Novitiate

THE EARLIEST governance structure of the new religious order was modeled on that of the Society of Jesus. Initially, one superior general would guide the various communities in different places. Unlike other orders of religious women, whose individual houses were independent, this structure would allow union among the different houses.

Although Fr. Varin considered Sophie the superior of the community, he guided her with a heavy hand. He still expected decisions to be sent through him, a practice that became less practical with increasing political tension in France. He even made significant decisions without consulting Sophie. First, while Sophie was in Grenoble, Fr. Varin appointed Anne Baudemont as the local superior in Amiens. Second, when a new community was established in Belley, Fr. Varin sent Henriette Grosier there. When these first three communities were established—Grenoble, Amiens, and Belley—Fr. Varin called for an election of a superior general to govern all three houses.

A power struggle ensued as different models of religious life clashed. Anne Baudemont came to the community in Amiens after some years in another community, and she was familiar with the traditional model of independent houses. Thus, when she was assigned as superior of the community in Amiens, she envisioned herself with the authority to make independent decisions. With the support of the community's confessor, Fr. Sambucy de Saint-Estève, she made significant changes without considering the needs of the communities with which she was affiliated. Because their understandings of governance differed, Anne's and Sophie's respective houses started to move in different directions. Anne retained many of the monastic practices that Sophie did not want, a practice emphasized when Anne and Fr. Saint-Estève wrote a new rule to guide the Amiens community while Sophie was in Grenoble. When Sophie brought her concerns to Fr. Varin, he dismissed them as coming from her inexperience. He asked her to trust him.

Sophie returned to Amiens in December 1805 to address two significant decisions: the name of the community and the election of a superior general. The name was chosen from Fr. de Tournély's original impulse: The Daughters of the Sacred Heart of Jesus.[1] They also agreed to base their future constitutions on those of the Society of Jesus. The second task that faced the small group was more challenging to resolve. When it came time to vote for the superior general, an office with the term of life, written votes arrived from the other houses, and the local community submitted their own. Sophie was elected by just one vote. Her election disappointed the local sisters, and the community spirit became strained.

Sophie stayed a few weeks under these difficult circumstances, and then she decided to return to Grenoble with a stop at her family home in Joigny. She was able to remain with her family and truly rest. Upon her return to Grenoble, she was warmly received, though others noticed that she was not completely well. She left Grenoble again in July 1806 to make two more connections with fledgling houses that sought affiliation with the Daughters of the Sacred Heart, ultimately landing in Poitiers. Along the way, Sophie experienced healing that left her feeling well for the first time in three years. She recounted it to Philippine in August when she arrived in Poitiers:

> You remember the state of my health when I left you? When I arrived at Lyons after such a tiring journey, I was worse than last year. Far away from my dear Samaritan, I could think of no one else who could cure me; she seemed essential to my physical well-being as she thought me necessary for the good of her soul. I complained gently to our Lord of the situation; a long journey and no one to turn to. After this I remained at peace, recalling all the kindness and love God had shown me previously. I had hardly left Lyon when all had disappeared, yet I had taken no remedy—on the contrary the excessive heat at the time, no chance of a rest, the poor food and dirty inns: everything should have made it worse yet in one night I was quite cured![2]

Sophie arrived at the monastery of Les Feuillants in Poitiers on July 23, 1806, in the midst of a rainstorm that left her soaked. Two women had been living there since 1802, trying to establish a school for girls as a way to help rebuild society. They found the work too much for them and were on the brink of signing the building over to the diocese. They discussed with Sophie the goals of the new order and agreed that the school and the religious community would become affiliated with the Daughters of the Sacred Heart. The local clergy also accepted the arrangement. Understanding that the bishop wanted her to consider Poitiers the center of the order, Sophie stated that it would become the novitiate and she would be there as much as possible.

The question of personnel to run the school was answered in part by yet another group of women seeking religious life.

Fr. Varin introduced Sophie to a group of six women in Bordeaux who were looking for a religious community. When Sophie arrived, she found that the women and their families expected the convent to be established there in Bordeaux. Unable to support the school in Poitiers without the help of these women, Sophie met with their parents and reassured them that she would return to establish a community in Bordeaux. She then interviewed about thirty women in addition to the original six, ultimately choosing eight to come to Poitiers for the novitiate. They traveled in small groups, Sophie going with Thérèse Maillucheau, the leader of the small group, to visit Thérèse's family on the way. Sophie reassured Thérèse's family, which also helped to reassure the families of the others who had opted to join Sophie's community.

The new recruits brought life and hope to the community at Poitiers. The school could now be run, and the community adopted a more prayerful lifestyle. In addition to Sophie and Henriette Giraud, who had accompanied her from Grenoble, there were ten novices, nine boarders, a cook, a shepherdess, and a gardener. Sophie was in charge of the novitiate, which opened on September 5, 1806. Under the neighbors' watchful eyes, the young women repaired the old monastery and learned to run the school.

The experience of the novitiate at Poitiers was recorded in the house journal Sophie wrote, and so we have a fuller image of it than Grenoble. The novitiate showed her the challenges young women faced, whether from their own backgrounds or the trials of religious formation. She herself learned to model the type of religious she wanted others to be. This challenged her to reflect on the lifestyle she learned while her brother Louis was controlling the household in Paris. The asceticism, especially around food and eating, was too severe to support the physical health of Sophie herself and her novices. Sophie gradually recognized that health must be preserved, and ascetic practices must be curtailed in order to support the sisters' ministry in the school. Sophie learned this through her own tendency to become ill. Awareness of her own needs and limitations in turn helped her respond to the needs of others around the daily routine of prayer, hard work, fasting, and spiritual reading.

The novitiate community at Poitiers strengthened their bonds by telling their life stories to one another nightly during recreation. To allow each one time to tell her story, Sophie placed a pin in the candle and allowed the candle to burn to the pin while the story was told. The drama of the Revolution with its heroism and losses bonded the sisters by candlelight. Friendship grew alongside their admiration for and reliance on Sophie.

Image 4. Our Lady of the Society.

Although she was still quite young, the education Sophie received from her brother and her experiences in Paris, Grenoble, and Amiens had prepared her well for leadership. As she fostered the community's growth, her own style of leadership started to shine. Personal relationships, clear communication, and prayerful discernment, evident in the experience at Bordeaux, became hallmarks of her manner.

The Poitiers monastery was ready for the school to expand by spring 1807, and Sophie decided to open a school for the poor. It opened at the end of 1807 and was running smoothly by June 1808. Its immediate success highlighted the great need of society at large.

5

Division at Amiens

THE SITUATION in Amiens was not going as smoothly as in Poitiers. Fr. Sambucy de Saint-Estève continued to dominate Anne Baudemont and the community. Baudemont and Saint-Estève composed governing documents without the knowledge of Sophie or Varin, both of whom were occupied elsewhere. Saint-Estève, who left the Fathers of the Faith in 1807, during a time when they were marginalized by the French government and suppressed, sought formal governmental approval in 1806 for the schools of the Dames de l'Instruction Chrétienne, one of the names by which the community was known. In a bid to look more favorable to the French government, he indicated that the Dames were no longer connected to the Fathers of the Faith, omitted Sophie's name and role as superior general for life, and omitted their connection to Fr. Varin, who was considered suspect by the government (as were the Jesuits). Napoleon granted formal recognition of the association in March 1807, and Sophie soon learned of it from Fr. Varin. Although she was not ready for the move, it assured compliance with French law and gave the association some legal standing to present to local authorities.

From June 1806 to October 1814, no letters between Sophie and Fr. Varin survive, and during this time the former Fathers of the Faith were restricted to their own dioceses. Sophie took in hand the leadership of three houses—Poitiers, Grenoble, and Niort—which opened in 1808. As superior general, Sophie also had authority over Amiens on paper, despite her inability to act there. Two more houses were added to the congregation in 1808 under the leadership of Baudemont and Saint-Estève, in Ghent then in French territory, and Cuignières. The community in Cuignières was opened by Anne Baudemont as a place to which the Amiens community could flee if they needed to escape the increasing scrutiny of the French government. Saint-Estève negotiated with the bishop of Ghent, to establish a boarding school and school for the poor in a former Cistercian abbey.

In July 1808, Sophie decided it was time to face the issues at Amiens head-on. She began a formal visit to the community. On the way, traveling with Thérèse de Maillucheau, Sophie stopped in Paris to meet with Mme. de Gramont d'Aster, a noble widow who sent her daughter, Eugénie de Gramont, to Amiens to study. Both Eugénie and her mother later entered the novitiate. While in Paris, Mme. de Gramont d'Aster introduced Sophie to Fr. Jean Montaigne, the rector of Saint-Sulpice. During these days, Sophie began to turn to him for spiritual guidance. She spoke to him of the foundation of the association and the challenges she was experiencing at the time. He responded to her, "there is a seed of destruction in your midst; but someone very powerful and close to God is praying for you and for your order."[1] That seed of destruction would become more evident throughout the coming years in Sophie's interactions with the community at Amiens. This time in Paris prepared Sophie to meet the difficulties that awaited her in Amiens, though she did not yet address the "seed of destruction."

Arriving in Amiens in August, Sophie found a large community and school. There were thirty-two members of the community, fifty-two boarders, and 140 students in the school for the poor. Anne Baudemont was the local superior and headmistress, and she and her assistants greeted Sophie with outward affection. They presented to her the successful community and school, seeking only for her to approve the way they were running the community. Recognizing its success, Sophie at first tried to adapt to their way of proceeding. Unlike Sophie, most of the women in the community were members of the nobility. The education they offered met a need, and it supported the members of their social class in the midst of the tumultuous sociopolitical climate.

In addition to their difference in social class, the local community told a different foundation story, which shaped their identity. They believed Fr. Saint-Estève was the founder of the community and Anne Baudemont its superior. Sophie and her ideas had no place there. Reading the situation, Sophie was not yet able to address the problems. For the next six years, she guided the other houses of the congregation, going as little as possible to Amiens and keeping the problems there to herself.

Fr. Saint-Estève continued to promote his image as the heroic founder of the house at Amiens. Heedless of the rule Sophie used at Poitiers, Saint-Estève finished his own rule for the community and presented it to the sisters in 1811. It reflected his goals for the community, including an emphasis on welcoming former religious who had been forced to leave religious life due to the Revolution. It centered on the work of education. Contrary to Sophie's vision, Saint-Estève's model of governance and life was patterned more on monastic life than on the active model Sophie preferred. It also limited the superior general's term to ten years, ignoring the Jesuit model that held that position for life as a way to foster unity among members. Finally, it reflected the spirituality of the Sisters of Notre Dame and the Ursulines rather than Fr. Léonor de Tournély's focus on the spirituality of the Sacred Heart of Jesus. The overall picture resembled pre-Revolution religious life more than Sophie's innovative vision.

Sophie arrived in Amiens in January 1811 to participate in the vote on the new rule. The professed members of the Amiens community accepted it on a trial basis on February 2, 1811. Sophie then took the rule to the other communities, presenting it without commentary throughout the coming months. In each place, the community rejected the document as inconsistent with the way of life they had been following. Ghent most clearly felt threatened by the loss of the superior general remaining in that role for life, which they believed gave stability and reflected the Jesuit impulses of their society. In the other communities, the rule was rejected by the professed members for different reasons, including the loss of Sacred Heart spirituality and the lack of emphasis on the Eucharist.

The union of the congregation was at stake, as membership polarized around the two differing visions of their goals and purpose. Central to this division was the question of governance and the term length of the superior general. Unity of governance would allow the community to grow and expand in an organic way while always being clear about their composition as one body. The division which faced Sophie was compounded by the difference of opinion between her brother Louis, who had become a close friend to Philippine and the community at Grenoble, and Fr. Varin. While Fr. Varin maintained his confidence in Fr. Saint-Estève, Louis became critical of the shift Saint-Estève was initiating away from the Jesuit model of governance and Sacred Heart spirituality. To Sophie's relief, Louis stepped away rather than contributing to the growing division.

Sophie found an opportunity to address the situation at Amiens when Saint-Estève was arrested on June 6, 1812.[2] Sophie prepared to assert her role in Amiens and to make some changes to the rule. She traveled to Paris in November 1813, where she handled the issues with the support of Fr. Varin and sought her advisor Fr. Jean Montaigne. She then met several times with Fr. Saint-Estève while he was in jail in Paris, beginning in December 1813. Sophie and Saint-Estève came to two significant agreements: he conceded that she was superior general for life, and he agreed to recognize her as the local superior at Amiens.

Sophie arrived at Amiens in January 1814 and found the community was divided internally. Although Saint-Estève had agreed to the changes in governance, the community in Amiens remained opposed to Sophie. As Sophie took on the role of local superior, Eugénie de Gramont, who hardly knew Sophie, became her assistant general and Anne Baudemont her treasurer general. They and the others in leadership roles of the household remained loyal followers of Saint-Estève and Baudemont.

Political tensions were also shifting in France. Pope Pius VII formally reinstated the Jesuits in August 1814, and the Fathers of the Faith sought admission to the Jesuit novitiate. Fr. Saint-Estève was released from jail in April and appointed secretary to the ambassador to the Holy See. Sophie, accompanied by Frs. Montaigne and Varin, met with him in Paris before his departure to Rome. They agreed that, after the congregation made modifications to the rule, Fr. Saint-Estève would attempt to get it approved in Rome. When Sophie and Fr. Varin met in July 1814 to modify Saint-Estève's rule, Fr. Varin finally realized that it was not aligned with his or Fr. de Tournély's original inspiration for the new order of religious women. He and Sophie decided to ask Fr. Julien Druilhet to help them start the new order's Constitutions from scratch, centering the order's spiritual life on the Sacred Heart of Jesus. This decision was a definitive step in solidifying the order's foundation and Sophie's role as superior general.

6

Sabotage

THOUGH SOPHIE and her companions had understood that Fr. Saint-Estève would only act on behalf of the congregation after the general council voted on the rule, Saint-Estève acted prematurely and went directly to the Vatican with his rule when he arrived in Rome in the summer of 1814. He wrote to Fr. Varin of his connections with bishops and the pope, and he began to look for a house for the association to open in Rome. As before, Fr. Saint-Estève communicated solely to Fr. Varin, removing Sophie from the role that even he had agreed was hers. She wrote promptly to him to temper his behavior:

> Allow me to make an observation in this regard. You have already submitted our rules for examination; perhaps, following on this, now you will seek formal approbation. Before proceeding any further would it not be prudent to wait until the final draft has been completed and accepted by a general council of the Society. Indeed, to respond to the general desire of all the houses, with the exception of Amiens, which is less demanding on this point, *all* would prefer to

> have the rule of the Jesuit Institute adapted as far as possible for women, particularly since France has regained its freedom.
>
> As soon as this final draft is completed and accepted by the Society we will send it to you and then you may submit it for examination and approval....There is yet another point with which you must comply, concerning the name which we will adopt for the Society. You are aware that the [name] *Sacred Heart* has been agreed on by all with, it could be said, a kind of enthusiasm. It would be quite difficult to gain acceptance of another...so you will readily understand that just as it is for the Society to submit its Constitutions to the Pope, it is also the responsibility to choose its name....This question of the name will be the concern of the general council as well as everything regarding the Constitutions. The outcome of this council will be sent on to you, as we agreed verbally before you left [Paris]....This is the only way that we can possibly take to restore and create *one body* in the Society.[1]

The strength of Sophie's leadership was made quite clear to Fr. Saint-Estève in this letter, and he responded by trying to assert his authority over the congregation in letters to Sophie, Fr. Varin and Fr. Pierre de Clorivière, the superior of the Jesuits in Paris. While Saint-Estève used anger and threats, the three in Paris worked together to uphold the congregation's interests. To counteract the damage Saint-Estève was perpetrating in Rome, they wrote to the Jesuit provincial there, Fr. Louis Panizzoni. Sophie's letter outlined the creation of the new order including the background information he needed to connect the Association des Dames de l'Instruction Chrétienne to their foundational vision. Varin and Clorivière wrote to Panizzoni separately, asserting their trust in Sophie and their support of her views. They also asked a secular priest to write a similar letter of support.

Sophie's account of the creation of the association included an explanation of the different views of the rule for the order and her good faith attempts to have Fr. Saint-Estève's rule adopted by all the houses. She wrote of trying to convince Saint-Estève that the changes determined by the General Council of 1815 were necessary to remain faithful to the life and spirit the order had been living for over a decade. She wrote of her surprise that he had moved forward with presenting his own rule to the pope and the Jesuits and that he was trying to obtain property in Rome for the expansion of the association. Sophie's appeal to Panizzoni begs him to convince Saint-Estève to cease his work to get his rule approved, for it would only cause greater division in the order in France, as the majority of the sisters living there would not accept it. In Fr. Varin's response to Fr. Saint-Estève, he rescinded the approval that had been granted for Saint-Estève to move forward by their conversation in June 1814 and rejected his claims of being the founder and primary guide of the new foundation.

Even with Fr. Saint-Estève in Rome in 1814, Sophie's task at Amiens remained nearly impossible. Her attempt to foster unity was thwarted by the circle of leadership at Amiens, who clearly remained loyal to Saint-Estève. He continued to communicate with them. When Sophie became very sick in 1815, her illness became a pretext to remove her from the main house in Amiens to a small cottage on the property, separated from the rest of the community. The novices were kept entirely away from Sophie under the guise of protecting her health and energy. They were taught the rule that Saint-Estève had written along with the foundation myth that held he was the founder of the congregation. In what Kilroy characterizes as "character assassination," the novices were taught that Sophie was sly and Gallican, not in line with the Roman church. Novice Marie de la Croix reported that although she didn't know what Gallicanism was, she understood that it was wrong.

While Saint-Estève's work to sabotage the association continued, so too did the work of Sophie and Frs. Varin and de Clorivière, seeking to tell the true story of its foundation. Madame de Gramont d'Aster wrote at length to the French ambassador to the Holy See, countering Fr. Saint-Estève's influence. She pointed out that the new order needed more time before they could establish a large house in Rome, as they were still consolidating their personnel among the houses already opened. Because of her noble status, her letter was more likely to have reached the eyes of those to whom Saint-Estève was talking, much more so than Sophie's ever could.

Meanwhile, control of the area of Ghent changed hands from France to the Netherlands in winter 1814. The community in Ghent opted to separate from the Association des Dames de l'Instruction Chrétienne. They accepted neither the rule of Saint-Estève nor the newer developments of the congregation. Their fear of Gallican sympathies and the encouragement of the local bishop led to a decision that each member of the community would choose for herself whether to stay in Ghent or to return to Amiens. The break occurred before the new year of 1815, and all the French members of the community returned to Amiens. All the Belgian members but one remained in Ghent. Sophie, after the stress with the Ghent community, became so ill that she expected to die and received the last rites. She remained weak and ill throughout the spring of 1815, staying at Amiens. As sisters returned from Ghent, the Amiens community remained tense.

Fr. Saint-Esteve did not give up his bid for power over the association. By the summer of 1815, his plans to open a house at the Trinità dei Monti in Rome had failed, and he was trying to open a smaller house. He wrote to Sophie under the pseudonym

Stephanelli, claiming to be well connected at the Vatican. He told her a new version of the foundation story and encouraged her to give in to Fr. Saint-Estève's success. He threatened her with the excommunication of the entire community if she did not follow Saint-Esteve.[2] When Sophie received this letter in August, she was at Cuignières, resting and regaining her strength. She consulted with Frs. Varin and Montaigne. She replied to Stephanelli in September, seemingly aware that it was Saint-Estève. She wrote as if he were anonymous and refused to reveal his identity. In the letter, she refuted his arguments and described the level of division that Fr. Saint-Estève had caused in the community by not accepting her authority as superior general. She asserted that Saint-Estève had not received permission to act in her name, so nothing he did was binding.

In the course of this correspondence, Sophie realized the importance of completing the Constitutions she had begun composing with the Jesuits in Paris. She wrote to Pierre de Clorivière, the Jesuit superior, to ask for Fr. Varin's assistance in completing the Constitutions. He agreed. In September 1815, Sophie returned to Paris to work with Joseph Varin, Pierre de Clorivière, and Julien Druilhet on the new Constitutions.

At the same time, divisions within the congregation increased as women from Amiens moved to different houses and spread their discord. Sophie's advisor Fr. Montaigne suggested that Sophie should visit each house and offer the members of the house the option of staying there under her leadership or leaving to join Fr. Saint-Estève's group in Rome. He told her to make sure that the local bishop in each place was aware of the division and would assert the proper ownership of the house. Tensions in Amiens heightened when two sisters, one of them Saint-Estève's sister, left without a word to their community and went to Rome to join Saint-Estève. Eugénie de Gramont, though she had helped them plan their travels, pretended that she was surprised by their departure.

However, she said she understood it and encouraged Sophie to follow their lead and accept the foundation Saint-Estève had established in Rome. While there were supporters of Saint-Estève in the other houses to whom he also wrote, none of the communities were as divided as Amiens.

The council of 1815 marked a big move toward unity, but the chaos caused by Saint-Estève still had to be addressed, both within the community and within the clerical hierarchy. Sophie asserted that her silence on certain issues was not a tacit approval of Saint-Estève's actions, but rather a way to keep the peace:

> My authority over the house at Amiens was rendered ineffective because Mr [Saint-Estève] de S[ambucy] took everything into his own hands here. For the sake of peace, I decided to tolerate what I could not prevent, hoping that time would reconcile minds and hearts. Two years ago, I believed that the moment for this had come....Then, in the desire for peace, I urged all the houses to accept Mr De S's Constitutions. That is why there are objections now to the opposition I have taken, as if I am contradicting myself, but my actions then [in 1813] should be seen as a painful sacrifice endured for the sake of peace.[3]

The actions of Saint-Estève caused difficulty for many years, even after the pope, recognizing his dishonesty and deviousness, finally removed him from Rome in 1825.

7

The Constitutions of 1815

IN THE FOUNDATION of the Society of the Sacred Heart, the writing of the Constitutions and their approval at the 1815 general council were a watershed moment. Sophie's vision, relying on the impulse of Frs. Varin and de Tournély, was finally able to take concrete shape, putting language around what the sisters had been living for fifteen years. Documents such as these clarify expectations as well as provide a vision of the ideal to which the community can strive. As Sophie had already discovered in presenting Fr. Saint-Estève's rule to the different houses, the membership knew and upheld the vision they were living, so the language chosen in writing the Constitutions had to fit reality.

Drawing on the original vision of Fr. Léonor de Tournély, the Constitutions adopted the name Society of the Sacred Heart in place of the Association des Dames de l'Instruction Chrétienne. The Constitutions describe the aim and spirit of the Society, the means of accomplishing its aim, and regulations guiding membership, formation, governance, finances, and spiritual practices. The aim of the Society is "to glorify the

Sacred Heart of Jesus."[1] The Constitutions continue: "Hence it follows that the spirit of this Society is essentially based upon prayer and the interior life, since we cannot glorify the adorable Heart of Jesus worthily, save inasmuch as we apply ourselves to study its interior dispositions in order to unite and conform ourselves to them."[2]

The first part of the Constitutions describes the type of people who are well-suited to be admitted to the Society, while the second part outlines the stages and methods of formation. Special emphasis is placed on capacity for the vows and the practice of virtues in imitation of the Heart of Jesus.

> In order...to enter into the spirit of their Institute... which proposes to them [novices] this Divine Heart as the centre and model of all virtues, they must consider it their most sacred duty and most sweet occupation to contemplate, study and know intimately the interior dispositions of the Sacred Heart with regard to obedience, poverty and chastity, in order to conform and unite themselves closely to them.[3]

The formation directors are to be chosen for their dedication to strive for these characteristics, and they are instructed to foster growth for each one, recognizing that each person has distinct needs and gifts.

Part 3 of the Constitutions gives four means by which the Society seeks to glorify Jesus's heart: the education of children in boarding schools; free education of poor children; retreats for people (especially women) living in the world; and necessary contacts with people outside the convent. In order to accomplish these means, the members must work toward the virtues described in the section on formation, they must receive the necessary training for their apostolate, and they should take reasonable care of their health. Because education is the first means of this work, the Constitutions provide several chapters of guidance for boarding schools and for the instruction of children who are poor. Sisters devoted to this ministry must

> always remember that it is principally by humility, gentleness and kindness that they will gain the hearts of their pupils; that they will bring the seeds of virtue which they have planted there to maturity; that they will gather with joy the fruit of their arduous labours. Let them therefore be filled with tender and sincere affection for their children, but let the true love they bear them be drawn entirely from the Sacred Heart of Jesus.[4]

Part 4 of the Constitutions concerns the governance of the Society, establishing the roles of the superior general and her council, the cardinal protector, and local superiors, and the use of financial resources. This section also describes the qualities of good leaders. They should be virtuous, with good judgment, wise discernment, and pure intention. They should demonstrate and promote exact observance of the Constitutions. Their work and prayer should always foster union, and the text warns about the dangers of division. Finally, the Society's perseverance

> will be found in the love of all for the Divine Heart of Jesus, and in their fidelity in honouring and studying It, knowing It intimately, and uniting themselves, as far as they can to Its interior dispositions....It is, in fact, from this Divine Heart that they will draw that spirit of humility, gentleness, simplicity and obedi-

> ence, which should characterize all the members of the Society.[5]

By November, the new Constitutions were ready for the community to see, and a general council was called to open on November 1, 1815. Two representatives from each house met in Paris at the convent of St. Thomas de Villeneuve in apartments owned by Madame de Gramont d'Aster, whose support Sophie relied on. The representatives of each house were the superior *ex officio* and one professed member of the community named by Sophie Barat, in theory the oldest.

For a month the council discussed the draft of the Constitutions and reflected on the foundational story of the Society. The initial impulse of Fr. Léonor de Tournély, including both the influence of the Jesuits and the spirituality of the Sacred Heart, was woven together with religious rules from other traditions and the best educational materials of the time. On December 17, 1815, the congregation voted to accept the new Constitutions. With this act of acceptance, the new congregation's name became the Society of the Sacred Heart of Jesus. In addition, they elected the officers of the Society. Philippine Duchesne was elected secretary general, and Sophie's election as superior general for life was reaffirmed. Additionally, the group chose to ask the archbishop of Paris, Cardinal de Talleyrand-Périgord, to be their ecclesiastical superior. The cardinal accepted and assigned his secretary Fr. Perreau to act in his name. The council defined the design of the habit and the profession cross. They also debated materials that Fr. Saint-Estève had sent for consideration and rejected them.

With Sophie's leadership confirmed, her first act regarding the membership was a circular letter to communicate the decisions of the council. She asserted the unity of the council under the title of the Society of the Sacred Heart and the adoption of the new Constitutions. In this letter, she clearly affirmed the centrality of the Sacred Heart of Jesus in the origin and purpose of the order. She told the official story of the Society's beginnings and its evolution and acknowledged the divisions that had been present.

> The task was to overcome this seed of disunity which had been growing among us for several years and which could have had disastrous consequences. All of us had to bond together and follow the same rule of life, in accordance with God's design revealed in the foundation of this little Society. The Society at its origin was essentially founded on devotion to the Heart of Jesus and must be so dedicated and consecrated to the glory of this Divine Heart that all the works and functions it undertakes are related to that chief purpose....Such is the glorious and attractive aim of our little Society: we become holy ourselves by taking the divine Heart of Jesus as our model, trying as far as we are able to unite ourselves to his feelings and innermost dispositions; and at the same time we dedicate ourselves to extending and promoting the knowledge and love of this divine Heart by working for the sanctification of souls.[6]

By the time of the council of 1815, the Society had 108 members with an average age of thirty-nine. Sisters came from a wide variety of backgrounds. A distinction between teaching sisters and coadjutrix sisters had also become clear; the schools would not function without sisters who could take on the nonteaching duties such as cooking, housework, and gardening. This division of labor among the members of the order reflected the social divisions in French culture, emphasized by the many members of the nobility who entered the order and the families from whom the boarding schools drew students. Sophie, however, was clear that the needs of the houses had to match the capacities of the women who were accepted for membership as both teaching and coadjutrix sisters, and she urged superiors to take care not to accept too many sisters who would not be able to teach.

8

The Move to Paris

THE COUNCIL of 1815 marked a turning point for the Society following tumultuous divisions. Sophie's attention focused on fostering unity through her presence at the various houses, at the same time responding to the calls for growth. Requests for teachers and new foundations far outpaced the growing number of sisters available to support so many institutions. A letter to a local superior highlights the tension Sophie felt: "You ask for three class teachers immediately, saying that you have only lay sisters which adds to your overwork. Three teachers all at once. That's a tall order! You know...class teachers are not trained in the dozens! I hope that Madame Grosier will be able to send you one and later we will prepare another for you....I see very clearly from your work list that you are all overworked."[1]

Following the council of 1815, Sophie's task remained to foster unity among the members of the congregation. The hurts and divisions of the years leading to 1815 would not be resolved overnight. Sophie had started working toward greater unity in Amiens before the council by drawing toward her the two leaders of that community, Marie de la Croix and Eugénie de Gramont. She called the two women to be in Paris with her, Marie de la Croix as a companion and Eugénie de Gramont as a delegate from the Amiens community. Daughter of her friend Madame de Gramont d'Aster, Sophie recognized in Eugénie the ability to persuade people. Sophie needed her support to resolve the issues in Amiens. Both women had been considering leaving the Society to follow Saint-Estève, who continued to stoke division. During this time, Fr. Varin told Marie de la Croix about the true foundation of the Society, a story which had been hidden from her during her novitiate.[2] While the council was in session, Marie de la Croix had a transformative experience in which she ultimately decided to follow Sophie and not Saint-Estève. When Eugénie visited her after two weeks, she revealed that she, too, had decided not to go to Rome to Saint-Esteve's new community. Following this decision, Marie de la Croix publicly apologized to Sophie for her role in spreading the discord at Amiens. Eugénie, whose role was much larger than Marie's, watched this happen and did not step up to admit her own part. Marie felt the sting of betrayal and humiliation, which she carried with her for the rest of her life.[3]

Following the general council, Eugénie de Gramont spoke frankly with Sophie about her acceptance of the council's decisions and that she would not join Saint-Estève in Rome. Eugénie also wrote a public letter to the community at Amiens, stating that she placed her full support behind the decisions of the council. This allowed Sophie to return to Amiens and begin the process of building relationships with more ease.

Madame de Gramont d'Aster, who had since followed her daughter into the Society and lived at Amiens, welcomed Sophie warmly when she arrived. She then recorded her approach to gaining some unity among the sisters of the community. Sophie spent the first days meeting with individuals before calling them together as a community. In her talks with them, she encouraged each one to consider how their lifestyle differed from the initial ideals they had when entering the community. She told them of the decisions of the general council and of their new name, the Society of the Sacred Heart, all without offering room for conversation. She then launched a novena in honor of the Sacred Hearts of Jesus and Mary in which they would consider the new Constitutions. The confessor of the community came on the second day of the novena, and the individual confessions of the community took three days. As these days continued, Sophie read the Constitutions aloud in community and offered commentary. By the end of the novena, each of the members of the community had spoken to her privately.

The next step of the process was that each individual had to publicly declare their decisions to follow the Constitutions and accept Sophie as their superior general. In preparation for this step, Sophie planned a retreat for the community in which Fr. Dubas, the community confessor, would hold two conferences a day and she herself would speak each night. Kilroy describes what happened next:

> One evening, as Sophie stood up to leave the conference room, one of the community publicly asked her pardon for the manner in which she had been treated in Amiens over the years. The tension was broken at last that evening and the rest of the community also asked forgiveness. Sophie was so taken aback that she had to sit down again, and it became clear to all present that she was deeply moved. Only then did the community glimpse some of the pain inflicted by the coldness and antipathy shown her over the years. She responded finally by saying that she did forgive and accept them, and that it was time old wounds were healed. They embraced her and a sense of joy and release pervaded the house. A great burden had been lifted from everyone. By carefully

> planning the process of reconciliation, Sophie herself had broken through into the hearts of the community and created warmth and life and a sense of hope for the future.[4]

The formal ceremony of acceptance of the Constitutions and Sophie's leadership as superior general was completed on February 29, 1816.

The process of enacting the decisions of the general council was less straightforward in Poitiers, where the local bishop was a devotee of Fr. Saint-Estève, whom he believed would be named the superior of the congregation in France. Additionally, the naming of a superior general for life over the entire congregation challenged the common practice of local bishops holding authority over the nuns in their diocese. Sophie's role was thus a threat to local hierarchical authority. The concerns of the local clergy were sent to Fr. Perreau, the delegate of the Society's ecclesiastical superior. Sophie consulted with Perreau in Paris to determine how they could respond. Perreau's response was to uphold the decision of the general council, which could not be challenged by a local bishop or clergy, even if they disagreed with it. They could allow the community to live the Constitutions without approving everything in them, or if they would not do so, the community would leave the diocese and go where they could live their Constitutions. While Henriette Grosier as local superior clashed with the local bishop, Sophie was able to smooth over the relationship between the diocese and the community there. As so often was the case, Sophie was able to find a way forward through meeting personally with the people involved.

Although the conflict at Amiens was calming, it was no longer suitable as the center of the Society. Sophie sought a fresh start by establishing a motherhouse in Paris, including a central novitiate and a school. Paris in 1816 was the capital of the Counter-Revolutionaries, who focused on education as a means to restore the country after the Revolution and the reign of Napoleon. The Society of the Sacred Heart had the potential to effect radical change through the education of women, and so Paris seemed an ideal center. However, creating a new community of novices and a school required carefully choosing members who would foster unity rather than carry forward old divisions. Against the advice of Fr. Perreau, Sophie chose Eugénie de Gramont to move to Paris and begin the school. While Sophie intended the novitiate to be separate from the school, in fact the two communities were in the same house for a time.

Sophie arrived in April 1816 at the house on the rue des Postes that had been acquired by Philippine in her role as secretary general. The community was composed of six women from Grenoble (three choir novices, one coadjutrix novice, and two coadjutrix postulants); and five choir novices and one choir postulant from Amiens. The women from Amiens came with Eugénie de Gramont. Josephine Bigeu was named the novice mistress. The living space on the rue des Postes was too cramped for the community, and boarding students were soon welcomed too. Philippine Duchesne, preparing for her mission to the New World, was there as well. The crowded community suffered an outbreak of illness that hit the school in September 1817. Two novices and three students died; Eugénie became ill and left the community for a time to convalesce elsewhere.

In the crowded conditions, Sophie and Eugénie shared a room, which fostered their growing friendship. Through their work on this common project and its challenges, they grew to depend on each other, so much so that they were very close friends for the rest of their lives. Sophie relied on Eugénie to establish the educational endeavor in Paris. Eugénie's remorse at believing Saint-Estève over Sophie turned into great affection for the woman. Their genuine friendship was reflected in hundreds of letters, often expressing affection for each other and concern for each other's health. Sophie admitted to Eugénie and Thérèse de Maillucheau that she was experiencing depression during this time. She felt a lack of spiritual companionship and guidance, and the trials of the previous years carried considerable strain. Each member of her elected general council was fully occupied in other houses, and so she felt little support in her leadership role, either.

The trust that was building between Sophie and Eugénie, founded on their close work together, caused problems for Sophie in the form of gossip in Paris. The gossip about their familiarity and affection for each other was spread injudiciously to the community at Grenoble in 1818 by Marie Balastron after a two-year stay in Paris. Sophie responded to Balastron's indiscreet comments in the house that she needed to work closely with Eugénie in the administration of the school and the Society, and that the space at rue des Postes was constrained. She advised her to keep quiet rather than speak negatively of other Society houses. Sophie also advised Eugénie to show less affection openly and to write to her with the forwarded mail rather than separately. She was afraid that others would be upset by what they perceived as favoritism and urged Eugénie to burn her letters after reading them. Others warned Sophie to be wary of Eugénie's friendship, probably in part due to her previous affiliation with Saint-Estève.

9

To North America

WHILE THE Constitutions of 1815 were still taking root, the Society continued growing. In March 1817, a house was established at Quimper, taking over an existing school that had been run by the Visitation nuns. Sophie purchased the chateau of La Ferrandière in Villeurbanne, near Lyon, in February 1819. A boarding school opened in March that year, and a school for the poor opened in July 1820. In Bordeaux, a widow running a school and orphanage became a member of the Society, bringing the school and orphanage with her. Many other requests came, and Sophie regretted that she could not answer them all. However, one more request could finally be fulfilled.

Sophie received letters asking for sisters to be sent to the missions beginning in 1815, and the first one she felt was possible came from Louisiana. Sophie's desire to fulfill what was needed in the world matched well Philippine's long-standing call to lands far away. Philippine had heard of the missions as a boarding student in the Visitation monastery in Grenoble. Philippine's hopes to become a sister and a missionary held through repeated disappointments, first the Revolution, and then later by the immediate needs of the Society in France.

However, under the encouragement of Louis Barat, she kept her dream alive. When Louis Barat met the bishop of Louisiana, Louis Dubourg, in 1816, he told him about Philippine and her desire for the missions. Louis Barat wrote to Philippine, telling her to get ready to go, and to Sophie about this meeting. Yet Sophie was not prepared for this agenda to be promoted in her Society. Dubourg visited Sophie in Paris in January 1817 and left believing that Sophie had agreed to send Philippine. However, after later consultation with Varin and Perreau, she was convinced that this was not the right time, for Philippine was needed more in France. When Dubourg visited again in May, he was surprised that the decision was reversed. At this point, Philippine threw herself at Sophie's feet in the presence of the bishop and begged to be allowed to go. Sophie relented.

Arrangements were made quickly for Philippine and a group of sisters to leave the following spring, 1818. Four companions were chosen to accompany Philippine for this monumental mission: two choir sisters, Octavie Berthold and Eugénie Audé, and two lay sisters, Catherine Lamarre and Marguerite Manteau. All four sisters were judged to be mature and strong enough for the expected hardships of the journey and the mission. When they had gathered to make their preparations in Paris in February 1818, Sophie named Philippine the superior of the little group and offered them encouragement for their task. The next day, February 8, Eugénie Audé made her final vows during the Mass, and the Blessed Sacrament was exposed for adoration, to mark the holiness of this day for the Society. After lunch, Philippine and her companions said their farewells to Mother Barat before boarding the coach to Bordeaux, where they were to await their Atlantic passage.

Weather delayed their departure longer than anticipated, and the five made a retreat during that time. They finally boarded the ship, the *Rebecca*, on Holy Thursday, March 17, and set sail on March 19. Their accounts of the two-and-a-half-month-long voyage gave lively descriptions of stormy seas and seasickness in a crowded ship, the first glimpse of new fish and plant life, and the camaraderie of the passengers and crew. They reached the mouth of the Mississippi River on May 25 and were guided from there by a pilot from New Orleans. They stepped off the ship on the Feast of the Sacred Heart, May 29. Eugénie Audé described their arrival in New Orleans:

> It was with the deepest emotion that we set foot on this soil which is for us, in the eyes of faith and the designs of God, the Promised Land. Mother Duchesne's heart could not contain its sentiments of gratitude. In spite of the marshy ground she knelt and kissed the very soil. Her eyes were wet with tears, tears of joy, the kind Father Varin desired for us. "No one is looking," she whispered to us. "You kiss it, too." If only you could have seen her face! It was radiant with joy that only the Heart of Jesus could inspire in a soul filled with His grace and bent on glorifying His Sacred Heart.[1]

The companions were welcomed into the Ursuline convent in New Orleans and enjoyed their hospitality until a steamboat carried them up the Mississippi River to St. Louis. Arriving there on August 29, 1818, they continued a bit farther to St. Charles, where Bishop DuBourg had arranged for them to establish a school in this frontier community of about five hundred families. They lived in a rustic house called the "Duquette Mansion," which consisted of a central room with six small rooms surrounding it. The doors and windows would not fully shut and the roof leaked. Here, they opened the first Sacred Heart school in the New World, in September 1818, with three boarding students and twenty-two children in the free school. From this first foundation, the Society expanded throughout North America and later to South America as well.

Image 5. Portrait of Philippine Duchesne.

Following Philippine's departure, Sophie fell ill again, and her illness lasted much of the year. She was exhausted, and Philippine's departure left her without the assistance of her secretary general. That role remained empty until the next council in 1820. Following a time of convalescence, Sophie returned to the pattern that was beginning to form for her: extended periods in Paris interrupted by visits to houses or places where houses would be established. In addition, she remained close to her family through letters and occasional visits.

10

Hôtel Biron

A CENTER FOR the Society in Paris that included a large boarding school and a novitiate required a suitable property, a need that was central in Sophie's mind as she began to plan for the 1820 general council. Urgent issues caused by the rapid expansion of the order had emerged, especially the educational philosophies and plan of studies.

In preparation for the council, Sophie requested several reports. First, each member was to write an assessment of the previous five years, to see what had been accomplished and how the order was living out its ideals. Second, she asked for an inventory of the personnel of each house, including their gifts and capacity, and whether they were available for mission work. The schools were asked to report on the students and their level of studies. Each house also had to provide income and expenditure statements, and an account of the condition of the house and property. The council would be composed of Sophie, the six who were elected general counselors in 1815, and the superiors of those houses not represented by these women. Philippine was invited to come from North America, though her presence was not expected.

Hôtel Biron

The council opened August 15, 1820, in the small rue des Postes house in Paris. The first issue that became apparent was the need for more space, as the school and the novitiate were growing rapidly. The Hôtel Biron, a mansion for sale on the rue de Varenne, seemed an ideal location, and the council decided to bid on it. It had been on the market since 1817, with a price tag beyond the capacity of the Society. When the owner heard that the Society wished to purchase it for educational purposes, she lowered the asking price. It was an enormous transaction for the Society regardless. The Hôtel Biron was built between 1728 and 1731 by a financier who wanted the finest home in Paris. The next owner built the Petit-Hôtel in 1738 on the property. After passing through several other owners, some of whom rented out the property, the Hôtel Biron became vacant in 1811. The location in the Faubourg Saint-Germain had political significance as well, as members of wealthy and noble families were returning to the area. It was a center of aristocratic life, a life that was part of the pre-Revolutionary ways.

Sophie requested financial support from the king through the connections of members of the community, particularly Eugénie de Gramont's uncle, the Duc de Gramont. The king gave 50,000 francs immediately and promised 50,000 more, in return for the right to name five pupils annually. Sophie borrowed the remainder from businessmen, promising to repay them by 1824.

While the purchase of the Hôtel Biron was underway, the work of the general council continued. Fr. Joseph Varin and others told the foundation story during times of reflection, including Saint-Estève's efforts to sabotage the order. All told, the Society had twenty years of history already. The council determined that the history of each house would also be recorded.

Image 6. The Hôtel Biron, on the rue de Varenne in Paris, purchased in 1820 and now the Rodin Museum.

A major task of the council involved the plan of studies. Several documents concerning education had been written between 1804 and 1815, and they were reviewed. The first plan of studies adopted in 1806 was modified slightly in 1810 and had been in use since then. A Jesuit who was influential in the first plan of studies of 1804, Nicholas Loriquet, spoke to the assembly. He had written the plan of studies adopted by Jesuit schools in France between 1805 and 1807. The council examined the Society of the Sacred Heart's plan of 1810 over three days and made only minor changes.

The plan of studies was useful, but it depended on the proper training of teachers. This issue was a constant struggle as the Society grew so rapidly and the schools were in high demand. Thus, the question of formation emerged. Though the novitiate was to last two years, that was not sufficient time to prepare a teacher, and often the novitiate was shortened as novices were placed in classrooms to meet immediate needs in the schools. House superiors and headmistresses needed to continue training the teachers beyond their initial formation. They could use individual guidance, by listening to the needs of newer teachers, and they could address particular issues in the weekly conferences held in their communities. Each school had different needs, and they required both Sophie's attention to address them on a Society-wide level, and their own appropriate local leadership.[1] The problems ranged from poor leadership, to a need for greater simplicity, to conflict with bishops who imposed new teaching methods that were deemed inappropriate for the Society. Some schools were in such demand that their classes were huge. Fees were charged only to boarders, and they did not include tuition—only room, board, heating, and other material needs. Some schools requested to take day pupils and ask a fee for their tuition, which Sophie granted as long as they were kept in different classrooms, as it was considered improper to mix social classes together.

The general council also passed legislation regarding cloister, limiting the reasons for which sisters could leave the houses. From now on, all works of the Society were to take place on the property. Additionally, the council determined that only properties that were large enough to accommodate a school and community and had significant grounds for a garden could be accepted. Additional rules regarding visitors and students and their access to different parts of the house were agreed upon. Fr. Varin presented a summary of the Constitutions, and it was determined that this summary alongside St. Ignatius's letter on obedience would be read each month in community. In order to seek formal recognition by the pope, the community would also need a Ceremonial describing the rituals and ceremonies of the Society. The final act of the council was to elect officials. Henriette Grosier replaced Philippine Duchesne as the secretary general.

Following the council, Sophie continued the plans to move from rue des Postes to the Hôtel Biron on the rue de Varenne. She identified the main building for the use of the school and began to simplify its interior extravagance. The community would live in the stables, where the servants and horses had lived before. The school and community moved in on October 10, 1820. In November, the Duchesse d'Angoulême and the Duchesse de Berry visited the school, giving it a mark of approval of the royalty, which was not an uncommon occurrence in schools of the time. This visit also had political implications for the Society of the Sacred Heart, identifying it as sympathetic to the Bourbons.

In the midst of her administrative responsibilities, Sophie also continued to write to her beloved friends with affection and spiritual advice. She wrote to Mother Thérèse Maillucheau in Grenoble on September 3, 1819:

> All that you told me has consoled me singularly; your good dispositions to fulfill your important mission more perfectly than ever; the efforts that you make to overcome your own character so as to be more kindly toward your sisters, finally that spirit of zeal that leads you to give yourself away, to be all to all, and even to watch closely over temporal matters, so essential to the good order and tranquility of a house; all that delights me, and certainly the Lord for whom you make the sacrifice of what you hold most dear, I mean the attraction that draws you toward solitude, the Lord, I repeat, will pay you back a hundredfold for what you give Him. Have complete confidence, then, in His goodness, and above all act calmly and with a holy abandonment.[2]

11

Gifts and Stresses

THE HÔTEL BIRON drew criticism from other religious orders for its opulence. Though the general council felt the decision to purchase the property was correct, as the space was sufficient for both a convent and a school, the impression given was that of wealth and excess. Even its location in the Faubourg St-Germain indicated an association with the noble classes. Louis Barat received a letter from Eugénie Audé in America, critical of the decision to spend so much money while in Louisiana they were living in utter poverty. Sophie wrote back to Eugénie that her criticism was misplaced and inappropriate. Later in life, she would reflect on the purchase of the Hôtel Biron with greater knowledge of the impact it had on the reputation of the congregation:

> Unfortunately we shall never be able to eliminate the disastrous impression spread throughout France and to other parts of the world, concerning our so-called extravagance at the beginning of the boarding school in Paris. The gilded mansion gave it this reputation and some teachers did not prevent the pupils from spending money needlessly. This unfortunate

> reputation still goes round the world and each year deprives us of a great number of pupils, to the advantage of other schools....So every time these pious people in society either see us or hear of us placing a value on worldly ways, on the nobility, on greatness, or if our conversations are not serious enough, religious, full of zeal for the salvation of all, then we are criticised, judged harshly and often people no longer respect us.[1]

This was not the first recognition of the Society's connections to the higher levels of French society: the reputation of the house at Amiens was shaped by Anne Baudemont and Fr. Saint-Estève's connections to royalty and nobility, and the lifestyle there was not marked by poverty. This reputation did not acknowledge that from the beginning the Society educated poor students who were unable to pay as well as upper middle class and the aristocracy. The innovation of offering education for girls brought ready criticism. Yet, the Hôtel Biron highlighted excess in itself. The appointment of Eugénie de Gramont as headmistress—a position she held for thirty years—drew even more attention, causing the Society to be associated with the wealth and position of pre-Revolutionary nobility. The opulence of the school and Eugénie's active fostering of the Bourbon connections caused worry for Sophie and scandal for the Society.[2]

Under Eugénie's leadership, the Hôtel Biron brought to Paris many of the characteristics and desires of the original community in Amiens. When she wasn't traveling to visit the communities elsewhere, Sophie lived at the rue de Varenne. She encouraged Eugénie to treat the members of the community equally, rather than snubbing some and favoring others. Sophie had to reprimand Eugénie repeatedly for her harsh treatment of young girls. Eugénie seemed to push them hard without allowing for the fragility of their youth.

As problematic as it could be, Eugénie's connections to the aristocracy also opened doors for the Society's expansion. The school at rue de Varenne grew quickly, coming to include day pupils when the room for boarders filled. Sophie's plan for a school for the poor there was never fulfilled, but the rue de Varenne and other schools soon opened doors for physically disabled students. This was not encouraged, as it was expensive. The boarding school was filled with privileged girls who came because they were attracted to the school's fashionable reputation. Early students noted the aristocratic tone not only among students but also among the sisters, most of whom came from old money and families. Ironically, the old families and aristocracy often were materially poor and unable to pay the fees required by the school.

The education at the rue de Varenne only loosely followed the plan of studies of 1820. Classes were frequently interrupted by visiting royalty or clergy, and emphasis was placed on devotions and religious practices. One student noted in her memoirs that the level of education was disappointing, largely preparing women for the traditional needs of marriage.[3]

The Society continued to grow rapidly. Between 1820 and 1825, new foundations were established in France at Le Mans, Autun, and Besançon; in Turin in Sardinia; and in the New World at Grand Coteau and St. Michael's. Additionally, two diocesan congregations requested to join from Metz and Bordeaux, and many of the community at Ghent who had separated in 1814 asked to rejoin. Kilroy describes the decision-making and implementation process:

> As a general rule, Sophie accepted, planned and coordinated the new foundations in the Society, but once a decision had been taken, she discussed

> its implementation with several key members of the Society, especially Catherine de Charbonnel and Josephine Bigeu, and these carried out Sophie's wishes, even though it meant they were away from either Paris or their own communities for long periods of time. Once a new house was ready to open then Sophie sent the nucleus of the new community, with a named leader, to begin the new work. As the foundations increased Sophie retained direct contact with them through the letters she wrote to each superior. These letters were her means of forming those in leadership, many of whom had no experience at all of what it meant to run a house, run a school and a community, deal with local secular and church authorities, give spiritual guidance and support, and, most of all, model and maintain the spiritual vision of the Society.[4]

In addition to the new houses, there were increasing requests for establishments and for women seeking admission, signs that the community was perceived as promising and growing. Membership in the Society could not keep up with the demand for teachers. Furthermore, finances were difficult to manage with such rapid growth. Catherine de Charbonnel became the bursar after the general council in 1820, and Sophie remained close to all the financial transactions. Income came from the legacies or income of members of the Society, fees from the boarding schools, and some gifts from wealthy lay patrons. The major expenses were building campaigns when schools needed to expand. Sophie avoided debt as much as possible but was flexible enough to obtain it when a promising new venture opened, as was the case with the purchase of the Hôtel Biron. She was also quick to close those houses that were not working out. Even so, she constantly received letters from local superiors asking for money and personnel. The mission in North America was also desperate for funding, which mostly came from the families of the French sisters and the Society in France.

In 1822, Grenoble, under the leadership of Thérèse Maillucheau and Marie de la Croix, came near bankruptcy and disaster. Neither Thérèse nor Marie had the financial intellect that was required. Sophie sent Thérèse to Quimper as superior of the community with no responsibility over the finances or the school. Marie remained in Grenoble as the superior, where the stress was too much for her, and she became ill. Sophie spent early 1823 in Grenoble reorganizing the house and paying off debts.

Following the end of Napoleon's rule, Sophie's family in Joigny suffered economic hardship and bad harvests. When the husband of Sophie's sister Marie-Louise died in 1820, she and her family were left destitute. Both Sophie and Louis encouraged their nieces and nephews to work hard to help the family survive. Sophie ensured that her nieces received a good education and kept track of their accomplishments. She wrote to them, gave them small gifts, and visited them when she was present in their boarding school. Sophie also attended to the nieces of other sisters who were in the Society's schools.

In June 1822, Sophie's mother passed away. Marie-Louise was left alone in Joigny, and Sophie provided some material help through the purchase of wine, fruit, and nuts from her sister. Three of her daughters had entered the Society, and her son Stanislas visited often. Her son Louis Dusaussoy had attempted to become a Jesuit twice but remained a secular priest. He was not quite capable of caring for himself, so Sophie arranged some chaplaincy work at the Society houses on occasion, both in Europe and America.

Sophie, too, became very ill, to the point of death. As news passed throughout the Society, her youngest niece heard about it at school in Amiens. Dosithée was fourteen, and when she contracted a fever, she asked God to take her life and heal her aunt's. On the day Dosithée died, Sophie's forty-five-day-long fever ended, and she was significantly improved.

Dosithée's death shows the depth of love and admiration Sophie received from her family and among the sisters in the community. This time of great expansion, accompanied by constant shortage of resources, caused Sophie and the Society a great deal of stress. While the major disagreements and divisions that had been so obvious at Amiens and with Fr. Saint-Estève seemed to have diminished, the internal organization of the Society was still in its infancy, and peace did not prevail. As with all things in this world, challenges coexisted with great good.

12

A Loving God

IN A LETTER during her illness, Fr. Varin encouraged Sophie to be more open about her struggles and worries, noting that it might help her to bear them. Indeed, she rarely opened her deepest self to anyone other than Fr. Jean Montaigne, who died in 1821. It was only in 1824 that Sophie found another trusted spiritual guide. Joseph-Marie Favre was a diocesan missionary trained in the theology of St. Francis de Sales and St. Alphonsus Liguori. Fr. Favre stressed frequent communion in his talks and urged priests to be quick to give absolution, rather than dwell on the sinfulness of the faithful confessing. This view of God further challenged the harshness of Jansenism and took Sophie's spirituality one step deeper, toward a warmer and kinder vision of God. In a letter to Sophie in 1824, he wrote:

> God is calling you to an intimate union with Him. You must overcome all that impedes this relationship. *YOUR CONTACTS WITH PEOPLE* are not the least of these obstacles. Keep them to a minimum and only when necessary. Let go of everything which does not absolutely require your involvement in the

exercise of your responsibility. By being united to God you will do more in a quarter of an hour than in a whole day's *pouring out* of frenzied activity. Neither is *ENTHUSIASM* the least of obstacles: restrain yourself and moderate your actions in such a way that you are more attentive to God than to the chaotic nature of your occupations, which, however necessary, are less important than your great spiritual ideal. Furthermore, your duty to God and to yourself comes before your duty to your neighbour. And you can only give out of what you have....Go to communion as often as you can; your poor soul needs it so much; every day would be best.[1]

Image 7. Embroidery created by Sophie Barat, symbolizing the Sacred Heart of Jesus and the Immaculate Heart of Mary. The original hangs in her family home in Joigny.

Fr. Favre's cautions to Sophie highlight key characteristics of her personality and way of living. She devoted herself to relationships to the diminishment of her own time with God, and she took on with vigor the unending responsibilities of her role as superior general. Favre encouraged her to rely on others to take care of the burden, and his work with her helped to shift her spirituality toward the God of love that is so characteristic of the Society of the Sacred Heart.

Favre's ideas about daily communion were not considered appropriate by the Parisian clergy and religious, for it made God very accessible to the people. Hearing criticism of his spirituality brought Sophie to doubt his guidance. He reminded her of the many changes that had occurred in her life and in her spiritual life since he had started guiding her. She had lost her way in her inner life and focused too much on the external needs of the Society and the successes it bore. Favre's guidance helped her to balance her spiritual life and ministry more appropriately. Louise de Limminghe and Favre formed a little community of spiritual support for Sophie, and they called each other nicknames: Favre was John of the Cross, Sophie was Madeleine of the Cross, and Louise was Addolorata, or Addo for short. Favre encouraged Louise to stop Sophie from doing corporal penance, a habit she acquired early in life that reflected a more judgmental image of God.

Though the Society was deeply rooted in France and now in Paris, with the aristocracy, royalty, and Faubourg St-Germain, Sophie's theology remained aligned with the papacy. Favre supported this alignment and helped turn Sophie's attention to the growing Society in Rome. Gallicanism remained strong in France, and along with it, the worry of papal encroachment on the French church. Sophie knew that the Society needed formal approval from Rome. This approval would establish the authority that Sophie needed as superior in the congregation, and it would allow for growth in dioceses outside of France. It would also (she hoped) finally end the interference of Saint-Estève. She opened the formal process with Rome in summer 1823. She did so secretly, aware that if Saint-Estève discovered this process he would do whatever he could to undermine it.

Fr. Favre worried that Sophie's distrust of God harmed her health. He advised her:

> Trust and the love of God gladden the heart, uplift the soul and make it capable of the greatest undertakings, whereas fear and mistrust depress and sadden the soul, shrink the heart, dull the spirit, ruin the health of the body and disturb rhythm of the spiritual life. God did not come down upon the earth to be feared but to be loved. How...can you mistrust a God who infinitely loves you, who wishes only for your health and happiness? How can you mistrust your dear, kind brother Jesus, who has suffered so much to save you, who has made so many sacrifices, so that you could share in his glory and his treasures?...How can you mistrust this loving and gentle heart that only wishes to be loved and to give love? Such mistrust can only come from the devil....Let it never be intentional.[2]

He warned her and Louise about her scruples. Fr. Favre and Louise arranged an order of day to help Sophie find balance, and Fr. Favre required that she take on no more penance. Sleeping enough and eating what was put before her would be penance enough, since it contradicted what she had learned about penance growing up. Fr. Favre additionally forbade her from making a general confession for the time being, taking on his soul the repercussions in heaven. These steps were expressly intended to help her deepen her inner journey in ways that her spiritual advisors had been unable to help her in the past.

A Loving God

Fr. Favre's care for Sophie's spiritual life reinforced her initial impulse toward a more loving image of God. While she generously shared that love with others, Fr. Favre expressed God's tender care for her, which she had more difficulty recognizing.

13
Vatican Approval

THE APPROVAL of the Constitutions in 1815, the establishment of Sophie as lifelong superior general, the General Council of 1820's work on the educational mission of the Society, and the movement of the Society's center to Paris all marked major steps in solidifying the Society's legitimacy as a religious order. Continued interest in expansion beyond France—first to America and then to other countries in Europe and beyond—demonstrated that it was meeting the needs of the world in a significant way. The next natural step was to seek formal approval from the Vatican, legitimizing the Society's nature and apostolate within the Roman Catholic Church.

Though the spiritual foundation of the Constitutions was perfectly acceptable by the institutional church, there were some modifications to be made regarding lifestyle. Congregations of women seeking approval from the papacy were generally expected to include strict adherence to cloister, meaning complete separation from "the world," and solemn vows. Sophie's vision included solemn vows, which could only be dissolved by the pope, but a looser definition of cloister so that the women could be working in the places most needed. This was an innovation to be sure, and one that was considered dangerous by those making decisions regarding religious congregations. The Society was not the first or only religious order asking for this type of structure, and the type of life desired was not dramatically distinct from previous forms of religious life. What Sophie really needed was freedom from the local bishops and the ability to move sisters from one house to another as needs changed. She was also asking for a monastic lifestyle in the house, which would essentially keep the sisters grounded in the holy realm and less in touch with the worldly influences feared by the hierarchy. Sophie understood that prayer and the interior life needed time and space to develop, and the cloister helped facilitate that.

The packet sent to Rome included the Constitutions, a letter of petition signed by Sophie, Josephine Bigeu, Henriette Grosier, and Eugénie de Gramont, and letters of support from the ecclesiastical protector of the Society and his delegate Fr. Perreau. Additional letters came from bishops throughout France.

The pope issued a decree of approbation in September 1825, but it was not as clear as Sophie desired, for it left the sisters in simple vows which could be dissolved by a local bishop. She felt this was not sufficient to retain the Society's aim and intent and to secure her authority as superior general. Additionally, individual houses needed to have clarity about her central role so that they were not required to make changes to their ministry or Constitutions at the whim of the local bishop. Sophie had a particular example of such difficulty in the establishment in Turin, where the archbishop did not consider them true religious because they did not make solemn vows and did not live in papal cloister. Josephine Bigeu, who was in Turin dealing with the situation, encouraged Sophie to make some concessions in order to free the house in Turin from the local bishop's control. Sophie reopened the petition in Rome, this time sending three religious, including Josephine Bigeu, to represent the Society there. The pope assigned three cardinals to review the case, and it was recognized that a compromise was needed. Religious of the Sacred Heart would not make solemn vows, because solemn vows required the context of papal enclosure, but they would make a fourth vow of stability that could only be dispensed by the pope. This decision, while it wasn't as strong as they hoped, did gain the Society official papal recognition.

Another decision made by the papal commission was to place the Society under the ecclesiastical authority of a Roman cardinal who would become the Protector of the Society of the Sacred Heart. This gave Sophie greater freedom in her role, but it also challenged the Society's French houses, as the French church sought freedom from the Roman hierarchy.

Sophie wrote a circular letter in August 1826 announcing the approbation received and announcing the general council to begin in September.

> What a mark of His love the Heart of Jesus has given the Society, my dear daughters, and how full of gratitude our hearts should be! Our Savior has certainly more right than ever to expect solid virtue from us in return for such a blessing; and this most undoubtedly consists in greater punctuality and generosity in keeping our rules. Each of us should, henceforth, make them her principal study, and often say, to encourage herself to observe them exactly, "I am sure of obeying the Church and of doing the Will of my God."[1]

The General Council of 1826 began on September 29. The purpose was to consider the modifications required by Rome and to review the progress, life, and mission of the Society since 1820. When the delegates gathered, the revisions had not yet arrived from Rome, which took time as they were being translated from Italian to French. While they waited, Sophie addressed an issue that had emerged from the French government. To retain judicial status in the country, women's religious congregations were required to submit their Constitutions to the government for recognition by January 1, 1827. A law promulgated in 1825 had given the French government significant power over religious congregations including the power to dissolve them. Sophie's advisors had mixed reactions to the new requirement. Her friend Msgr. Frayssinous, minister of ecclesiastical affairs and public instruction, encouraged her to move forward with this process as a way to gain official recognition and further status in France. Other advisors, including Fr. Perreau, feared it would give the government too much control over the congregation. She agreed with bishops she consulted who suggested gaining the government's support would lend stability to the Society.

As the council debated this issue, the tension between the approbation of Rome and governmental recognition became evident. The influence of outside governments on the French congregation would likely be seen as threatening to the French government, while the congregation's missions in other lands were a great advantage in the recognition by Rome. When Sophie sought the advice of Fr. Rozaven, a Jesuit advisor in Rome, he "replied that the pope did not interfere with the laws of other countries and on balance it was better to conform to the requirements of French law."[2] With all these opposing points of view in mind, Sophie proposed that the Society comply with the French law, and the motion passed by a large majority. The Society's Constitutions were presented to the government of France in November 1826, and they were accepted, receiving the royal ordinance of authorization in April 1827.

The rest of the agenda of the council emerged from the concerns and matters brought forward by the other leaders of the Society. They examined personnel resources and needs, finances, spiritual life, and the educational mission of the members and the houses. One seemingly minor question was posed: whether the Society could take up education of the middle class. The decision was made on October 10, 1826, that this was not possible at the time, and the focus would remain on the upper middle classes and the poor. Though this was a decision made at the council, the schools with day pupils continued to educate them. Effectively, this decision kept the distinction among classes in the Society's schools.

The work of the council was done with the exception of the ratification of the Constitutions. Sophie suspended the council until March 1, when the Roman changes to the Constitutions were discussed and approved. The final act of the council was the election of officers on April 7, 1827. By this point, there were nineteen houses of the Society. Le Mans, France, and Grand Coteau, Louisiana, opened in 1821; Autun in 1822; Besançon, France, and Turin, Piedmont, in 1823; and St. Michael's, Louisiana, in 1825.

Rome's approval of the Constitutions was accomplished in part through Sophie's advisor, Fr. Jean Rozaven. Fr. Rozaven was the Jesuit assistant general for France, living in Rome. Previously a Father of the Faith, he entered the Jesuits in Russia while they were suppressed elsewhere. When they were reinstated universally (and suppressed in Russia), he returned to France. Then, elected as assistant general, he moved to Rome and lived the rest of his life there. Though he supported the Society of the Sacred Heart in many ways, he was critical of the role of education for women, preferring the traditional view of women's roles as modest and relegated to the private sphere. He wrote about the Society's ministry:

> I can see no necessity, nor useful purpose in a young girl, whose shyness and reserve ought to be her

> attraction, appearing in public and speaking with ease in the presence of one hundred or more people, only one of whom is her mother. All that she can gain from this are vain plaudits for which she will pay dearly, if as a result her modesty should suffer and vanity find a place in her heart. I do not like when a young woman draws attention to herself. I would rather that her merits were ignored or remained unknown, except by those on whom she relies for her own happiness....However I am assured that Madame Barat's establishments achieve much good in France and I believe it. But I doubt that this good will last.[3]

It was through Fr. Rozaven that Russian Princess Elizabeth Galitzine entered the Society. Elizabeth was born in 1795, and her father died when she was only four years old. Fr. Rozaven instructed her mother when she secretly became Catholic, and Elizabeth's conversion soon followed. When the Jesuits left Russia in 1815, Elizabeth continued to receive spiritual direction from Rozaven through letters that reveal the intensity of her spiritual experiences. When Elizabeth decided to become a religious, she asked Rozaven to choose an order for her, and he chose the Society of the Sacred Heart. Rozaven himself advocated to Sophie for Elizabeth's entrance into the Society in 1825, and he controlled some of the aspects of her religious life, including where she would enter and how she would administer her fortune. Sophie and Elizabeth exchanged several letters in anticipation of Elizabeth's entrance into the Society. Sophie's letter of October 2, 1825, shows her tender spiritual guidance of the princess:

> Do not distress yourself about the difficulty and the repugnance you feel sometimes for your prayer.

> Hold to the time you have fixed for it; beg pardon for your distractions and your longing for the time to be up, but don't cut it short by a minute....I desire so much to see you make great progress in the solid virtues of religious life, so that in this way you may respond to the great love which Jesus has for you. How immense his love is! It will call for boundless self-giving on your part.[4]

Elizabeth's acceptance to the novitiate soon followed. Sophie wrote: "So you will die of joy, my dear daughter, for I give permission for you to receive the habit on the day the Bishop chooses. Let me tell you, to restore the balance, that it brings great and awesome obligations."[5]

Sophie's vision of the Society and the role of the Religious of the Sacred Heart, guided by the Holy Spirit, is clear from a conference she gave in June 1827:

> A soul that is given over to the Holy Spirit no longer walks; she flies. The greatest sacrifices no longer cost, the roughest crosses no longer weigh her down. What am I saying, my daughters? The cross is her joy; she loves it, she desires it, for God allows that a soul that is thus given over, yielded up to Him, feels only the consolations instead of the pains of the cross. It is very different for weak souls who do not know the sweetness of the cross and who find only afflictions and thorns that tear them; the Holy Spirit makes a soul that has surrendered find flowers under the thorns.
>
> Who can say, dear daughters, what goes on in souls who are thus given over to the operations of the Holy Spirit? You see it in the lives of the saints that you read every day. If you read their letters,

> you will see how, in the midst of their difficulties, of the hardest kind of work and of incredible sufferings, they were filled with consolations, and said to themselves that they would not exchange their poverty and suffering, their crosses, for a more secure lot. And why? Because they had given themselves over entirely to God; they had kept back nothing of themselves, and the Holy Spirit filled them with His gifts.[6]

Sophie relied on Fr. Rozaven to assist the Society as it expanded into Italy and gained the approval of the pope. The strength of his opinions and the direction of his advice were not always the path she saw was best for the Society, and at times she ignored his directives. His relationship with Elizabeth Galitzine as her spiritual guide and protector also elicited instructions to Sophie regarding Elizabeth's formation. Sophie routinely had to place the needs of the Society as a whole in the forefront.

Vatican approval of the Society's Constitutions and increasing activity in Rome exacerbated the division in the French order between political and ecclesiastical factions. French strongholds felt threatened by the authority of the Vatican, and those aligned with Rome (the Ultramontane faction) saw the Gallicanism of the French church as incorrect. The centuries-long Gallican/Ultramontane conflict gave the internal union of the Society its fragile complexity.

14

A House in Rome

THE FORMAL approbation of the Constitutions in Rome helped draw together the far-flung members of the new Society of the Sacred Heart. However, the strain on Sophie's health was too much, and she was ill with a fever from December 1827 until the next summer. In one of her letters that month, she wrote,

> Help me by your prayers, my daughter, and do not cease to ask the Heart of Jesus for spouses simple, humble, full of zeal for the interests of His glory. How we need them! Work presses on us and becomes more demanding every day. For charity is growing cold; hearts do not yield themselves to divine love as in past ages. Let us at least rekindle it! The Heart of Jesus, that burning hearth-fire, can He not produce these sweet and strong effects in the souls consecrated to Him?[1]

During this time, the death of one of her early companions and an assistant general, Josephine Bigeu, left Sophie missing both her administrative help and friendship.

A House in Rome

Requests for sisters and new foundations continued to come to her. The Council of 1826–27 decided that new foundations would only be established if financial support was guaranteed by the local government or patrons, a decision to aid the financial stability of the Society as a whole. Houses in Lyon and Lille were opened in 1827 under these conditions. Then in January 1828, Sophie learned that Pope Leo XII wanted the Society to open a school in Rome to provide education for the girls of wealthy families in the Papal States. Such a school had been discussed for years, and Fr. Rozaven and others were working toward it, but Sophie was surprised by the pope's request. It was suggested that the former monastery of the Minimes at Trinità dei Monti, owned by the French government but abandoned since the French Revolution, would be an appropriate site. Negotiations led to an agreement that the Society could use the building, with strict rules and limitations that asserted the interests of the French government would be upheld.

The establishment of this school helped the Society make stable and valuable connections in Rome. At the suggestion of her ecclesial advisors, Sophie named Marie-Louise-Armande de Causans the superior of the new community, moving her from Turin. Sophie knew that Armande was charming and graceful with important people and yet also inefficient in dealing with the internal needs of a household. Armande took with her a small community to tend to the needs of the building, so long deserted. They moved into St. Sylvester convent, a cloistered Franciscan community, while they repaired the new home. Some months later a complete community would be sent so that the school could open. The strict cloister retained by religious women in Rome was far different for the French women, accustomed as they were to greater freedom of movement. The business negotiations that Armande had to complete were disruptive to the Franciscan community at St. Sylvester. Fr. Rozaven became a reliable support for Armande and the community, assisting them while they learned Italian and helping them navigate the Roman political realm of the Vatican and the ecclesiastical hierarchy.

Many of the decisions made in Rome were entirely in the hands of Armande de Causans, for Sophie knew that it would be difficult for her to understand the situation in Rome from far away. Sophie's leadership often allowed the local superior freedom to act in accord with local needs, as is seen with Philippine and others in America. Yet, Sophie remained overwhelmed by the weight of her office and the financial situation of the Society, especially the issue of debt. She wrote to Eugénie Audé in 1826:

> How tortured I am…being unable to give each of you immediately the amount you need. If you knew our difficulties and my endless worries over heavy debts which we still have despite my care and continual recommendations….I tell you now (only you and Madame Duchesne) that I have decided that if the Assembly (general council) which is about to take place does not adopt the strictest measures to reduce these debts, which have increased by 200,000 frs in the past year, I will resign as superior general. I do not wish to see the Society perish through lack of order and because we did not wish to economise. What nights I have spent! What constant worries I carry in my soul![2]

The French government's stipulations for use of the convent at Trinità dei Monti proved difficult from the beginning. Only French women could reside at the school, which made it difficult to provide enough teachers. Students had to be French and from the noble class, so the first group of students was very small. Because parents residing in Rome wanted their children to learn Italian, the foundation had to request special permission from the French government for an Italian teacher to reside at the school. Other jobs needed to be done, and there was not always a French woman to fill them. It became clear that another house would be needed for the Society to establish itself in the Papal States, for they needed a novitiate that could accept Italian women. Armande asked the pope that a school for poor children be established with the novitiate, a ministry that both fulfilled the purpose of the Society and was fully supported by the new Constitutions. A school for the poor in Rome needed Italians to run it, and thus the novitiate would sustain the work. In addition, there were already two benefactors ready to support this new apostolate.

Image 8. The Spanish Steps and the Trinità dei Monti in Rome, where a community was established in 1828.

The new community arrived in Rome in August 1828, led by Catherine de Charbonnel. Sophie wanted the new novitiate community to be in place the coming year, and she struggled to find the right leader, one who was prepared for leading the novices and who also spoke Italian. She articulated this general concern for the particularities of community in a letter of October 17, 1828:

> We don't live with angels; but with human nature which we must learn to understand and make allowances for. You know it only too well, but those in whom you see these real faults and limitations are far from recognizing them themselves, and so are deceiving themselves. In such cases and for the sake of peace, I try to see things through their eyes. It would be useless to turn on a more searching light, as it would not convince them. So I just wait![3]

In the meantime, Pope Leo XII died in 1829, his successor only lived two months on the papal throne, and Gregory XVI was elected in 1831. Sophie herself left France to visit the new properties in October 1832.

At this point there was a crisis of personnel, limiting Sophie's ability to open houses. New members needed time to develop their spiritual lives and to be trained to meet the needs of the Society, and some simply did not have the capacity for the type of work that was needed. Sophie's expectations were very high, and many recruits never measured up. Novices needed time to learn and grow, and the community needed time to figure out where their gifts were most appropriately used.

The role of the superior of a community was particularly demanding. Not only did she need to provide spiritual direction for the community but she also needed to administer both the house and the school, making personnel and business decisions. On her rested any negotiations with outside businesses, government officials, and clergy, where she was expected to protect the interests of the Society. In addition, she made the decisions on whom to admit to the Society and how they could best contribute to it. Kilroy writes,

> In a very real sense, the quality of personnel in the Society depended on the judgment of the local superiors....In the context of the role and place of women in nineteenth-century Europe, Sophie Barat's expectation and real need for such gifted women was a high ideal, and she found that if she wanted such women, she had to train them herself.[4]

Sophie guided the local superiors through her letters, and she was usually very transparent with them. She rarely consulted individual members but worked through the local superiors instead. When she became aware of an issue with a local superior, usually through gossip, she went directly to her. Sophie's genius was in her ability to recognize and foster the gifts of others and to shape women into leaders according to their needs and talents. This particular knowledge and formation of each local leader helped hold the Society together around the person of Sophie Barat, united in common purpose as well as personal friendship. However, it also made it difficult for Sophie to remove or change a local superior once they had been trained and established in a particular community.

Though the 1815 Constitutions called for a common novitiate, intended to be at the rue de Varenne, that proved to be impractical. Instead, each house was allowed to welcome and train novices. The unity of the Society would be greater served by a common novitiate, but there were too many novices to be accommodated in Paris. Because of the need for many noviceships, Sophie started to write to local superiors about their role in admitting women to the Society. Sophie herself gave permission for women to make their final vows, and she found that some who had entered years before were not really a good fit for the Society. Unsuitable candidates for religious life in the Society did more harm than good, and Sophie urged superiors to look for certain characteristics among the women who presented themselves for entrance. Writing to Philippine Duchesne, Sophie said, "We have a number who turn out to be useless through lack of talent and virtue, because each superior over a period of years has accepted all who asked to enter. In conscience we cannot send you any of them. Thus, we have a real need for new candidates whom we will train properly and who at the very least will have a sound vocation."[5] In addition, Sophie lamented that many young women died early.

Sophie's health continued to suffer. In 1829 she wrote that she fell seven times during the year, including once in April, hurting her right arm, and once in May, severely damaging her foot. By the end of the year, she was forced to stay in a basket chair that was carried by others. Doctors in France were unable to help her, either to relieve her pain or to set her foot properly. To add to the difficulties, another revolution was brewing in France.

15

Growth amid Turmoil

POLITICAL TENSIONS once again began to disrupt the growth of the Society in the late 1820s. When Charles X took the throne in 1824, the balance of power was shifting to the ancien régime, who longed for a return to the ways of the past. Because of the Hôtel Biron's location and clientele, the Society became associated with the nobility and the royal court. The Jesuits were on the brink of expulsion from France once again, and Sophie worried about the repercussions for the Society of the Sacred Heart.

Though she was physically incapacitated, Sophie planned for the likely possibility that the Society would be expelled from France. The Jesuits were expelled in 1828. The marquis Théodore de Nicolaÿ, whose daughters attended the Hôtel Biron, decided to move to Givisiez in Switzerland, and he provided Sophie with her contingency plan. He offered Sophie accommodation with his family there if the Society was forced to leave Paris.

The unrest in Paris became too much in July 1830. Sophie, now age fifty, was convinced by Eugénie de Gramont and her counselors to leave Paris on July 28, and the group left for Conflans, to the northwest of Paris. They returned to the rue de

Varenne on July 31. Just a week later, Sophie decided to move the community to Switzerland and take up the marquis's offer while searching for a more permanent solution. The novitiate community was dispersed among different houses. Sophie was in poor condition by September, and she spent about a week in Aix-les-Bains to rest and take the healing waters. Eugénie and Sophie arrived in Switzerland in October, where they found a location for the novitiate. Novices began arriving there from their dispersal in November.

Eugénie de Gramont and the archbishop of Paris, Hyacinthe de Quélen, found the new political situation in Paris impossible to accept. Archbishop de Quélen's palace was destroyed, and he took up residence with various religious orders throughout the city, including the rue de Varenne. Sophie knew that Eugénie was unhappy with the new political system, and she wrote to warn her about her behavior. She cautioned that Eugénie should not speak freely about political issues. Based on this admonishment, Eugénie believed Sophie accepted the new political situation, and a new tension emerged in their relationship. Yet, Sophie believed her role required her not to speak out on either side of the political debate. She later wrote of this issue:

> For what concerns civil government our role is to keep quiet, wait and pray. Ah, my daughter, what unhappy times for the Church! How she is torn on every side and persecuted by her own children! One thing should fill our minds, should possess us entirely: the desire to make up to the Heart of Jesus for so much ingratitude, and consequently every moment should see us grow in His love and in the hatred of our faults, so as to draw down His mercy on the souls that are entrusted to us.[1]

Still ailing, Sophie spent time in 1831 in Chambéry and Aix, receiving treatment for her foot during the week and catching up on mail and regular duties on the weekends in the community in Chambéry. She remained in contact with her spiritual guide, Fr. Favre, who encouraged her to integrate her ministerial duties and her interior life. Sophie often received news of Paris and the rue de Varenne from her brother Louis, who served at the school and community as confessor. He kept her informed that Archbishop de Quélen was present there very often. Without realizing this would become a source of scandal for the school and for the Society, Sophie recommended that Eugénie ask de Quélen to be her spiritual guide. Her correspondence with Eugénie continued, and their misunderstandings only grew. Eugénie proposed allowing Archbishop de Quélen permanent use of the Petit-Hôtel, a smaller building on the grounds of the Hôtel Biron, which surprised and discouraged Sophie. For all of Eugénie's ability to relate to the noble classes, she could not see the danger of this action.

When Sophie decided to leave the healing waters to return to Paris early because she felt isolated and alone, Eugénie thought she was expressing distrust in her leadership. Sophie responded in a letter that she had dramatically misunderstood her intentions and that the community there only sent her positive messages about Eugénie's leadership. Regardless, expressions of concern for Eugénie's wellness had reached Sophie. Eugénie could not help but think they criticized her to Sophie, and the relationship between the two became more tense. The tension emerged in a letter from Sophie in which she felt blamed for everything that happened to Eugénie: "So it is my fault for being ill! It's my fault that I can't walk! It's my fault if I don't go [to Paris]! Soon it will be my fault if the cholera strikes! Really, it's a case of the vanquished paying the penalty. Nevertheless, I hope you do not doubt my eagerness to see you, though you have spoiled it for me somewhat!"[2]

Sophie planned to stay in Paris only a short time, and then to take Eugénie to Rome with her to visit the Trinità in 1832. She set off from Chambéry and Aix toward Paris in October 1831, stopping in Joigny to visit her sister Marie-Louise and her nieces and nephews. Arriving in Paris later in October, Sophie continued to exert power over the community, though Eugénie largely ignored her wishes and even the consultations of the local community at the rue de Varenne. Sophie again began to feel out of place there, reminiscent of the early years at Amiens.

A devastating outbreak of cholera hit Paris in March of 1832, killing many though largely sparing the Society's houses. Archbishop de Quélen's activities among the sick and dying were recounted in the newspaper very positively. Sophie was heartbroken by the epidemic, and she suggested that the rue de Varenne could welcome orphans and care for them with the support of the community. Eugénie agreed immediately, and the cause gained the support and patronage of Archbishop de Quélen. In reading Eugénie's letter, it became clearer to Sophie that de Quélen was residing in the Petit-Hôtel despite Sophie's desires.

In May 1832, Sophie had received the recommendation of multiple doctors that her foot had so deteriorated it would need to be amputated. Louise de Limminghe connected Sophie with Mr. Rossi, a talented surgeon of the court, and he discovered that the ailment could be helped by wearing a bandage. Indeed, after several weeks of the bandage, the foot began to heal and Sophie was able to walk again, after four years on crutches or in the basket. On her recovery, Sophie decided to go directly to Rome rather than spend time in Paris catching up on her work. By this time, Eugénie and Archbishop de Quélen were actively keeping secret his residency at the Petit-Hôtel.

New houses were continually being established during this time. The house in La Fourche, Louisiana, was approved in

1826, as was the reopening of the house in St. Charles, Missouri. A foundation was started in Perpignan in 1828, and Sophie saw it as a gateway into Spain. With the knowledge that Ste. Marie-d'en-Haut would soon close due to city government forces, Sophie decided to open a house in nearby Avignon. Additionally, smaller communities sometimes asked to become part of the Society. One of these was a small foundation that began in 1800 at Annonay in Ardèche. They had desired to become devoted to the Sacred Heart, and their foundation included both a boarding and a day school. Similarly, in 1830 a request came from the bishop of Tours to incorporate the Community of the Holy Spirit into the Society. Sophie retained contact with the group until the time was right for their incorporation in 1836. Yet another community joined the Society in 1832, this one in Aix-en-Provence. Both the needs of the world and the reputation of the Society encouraged continued growth.

Image 9. Students and nuns at the Academy of the Sacred Heart in St. Charles, Missouri, USA, c. 1873.

16

Hardship in America

SOPHIE WROTE a circular letter to the Society in September 1832 in which she spoke of the healing of her foot, her visit to Rome, and the convening of a council to be held in Paris in 1833. She called for each house to prepare their accountings and reports on finances, personnel, and community life to be ready well in advance of the council. She arrived at Trinità dei Monti at the end of October 1832, once more temporarily hobbled, this time by a burn to her foot. Fortunately, it healed by the spring. While in Rome, Sophie saw to the second foundation there, establishing it in the Trastevere at Santa Rufina. She continued the study of Italian that she had begun while convalescing in Aix. By May, the work at Santa Rufina was completed and the novitiate began moving from the Trinità. Sophie made a final courtesy visit to the pope and left Rome in early June. She also met Fr. Jean Rozaven for the first time, greatly appreciative of all the support he had offered her during the approbation of the Society's Constitutions and the foundation of the Trinità. She was starting to recognize his influence over Elizabeth Galitzine. At this time, Jesuits were asked by their new superior general to distance themselves from communities of women religious. While members of the two orders had previously been very close, new appointments would make that more difficult moving forward.

Sophie left Rome in June. She arrived in Chambéry on July 17, 1833. She had a retreat led by Fr. Favre, and then composed a letter to the Society reporting on her visit to Rome. The council opened in Paris on September 29, 1833. As in the previous councils, Fr. Varin spoke about the history of the Society up to the present. The other work of the council included writing a directory of rules and instructions, to supplement the Constitutions that had been approved by Rome. The most pressing issues addressed by the council were the issue of quality education and the situation of the Society in America.

The quality of education was a recurring question. Sophie long lamented the lack of good teachers and the lack of time to properly train them. The council began by examining the plan of studies, proposing some changes, and hearing advice from Nicolas Loriquet, the Jesuit who had advised them at the previous council regarding the plan of studies. One concern brought to the council from parents was that their daughters were learning to be snobbish and to have expensive tastes, and that made them difficult at home. Louise de Limminghe suggested that the members of the Society remove the *de* from their names, which would denote a move away from nobility. The council debated the issue; however, the action was not taken because it would cause doubt in the courts for anything that had their legal names attached.

In North America, the Society needed greater guidance. The 1826 Council decided to assign an assistant general to America, but the decision was never implemented. Philippine kept Sophie well-informed of the community and their growth and circumstances in the New World, and Sophie paid careful attention, offering advice and money as she could. The differences in culture, language, geography, and sociopolitical context could hardly be overstated. The poverty and austerity lived by the sisters in the New World was extreme, and not everyone was capable of the lifestyle.

Members of the Sisters of the Cross in La Fourche asked to join in 1827. Because the sisters living there didn't know French, it was difficult to consider what to do. Sophie instructed Philippine how to carry out the joining of the community: that each member would be accepted individually and go through the novitiate, to become coadjutrix sisters. The work of the boarding school and the school for the poor there was carefully delineated from the work of the houses that catered to upper class students, and while La Fourche became part of the same work of St. Michael's as a sort of extension, the standards and expectations would remain separate to reflect the differences in social standing present.

In her first letter to the sisters in America, Sophie reaffirmed the authority given to Philippine over all the houses there. Though this was the case, guidance of those houses far from Philippine's own residence was hampered by the difficulty of conveying messages by post, and the length of time it took was prohibitive when the questions needed immediate answers. Sophie continued to receive and answer letters not only from Philippine but also from the superiors at St. Michael's and Grand Coteau, both in Louisiana. Sophie began planning a new foundation in New York, a way to consolidate some of the work in America and promote uniformity.

Following the council of 1827, Philippine made a formal visit to Lower Louisiana in 1829. Though Sophie had advised keeping the two schools separate in St. Michael's and La Fourche, Philippine's visit highlighted the issue of social status in North America. American culture was not stratified like French society was, and Philippine wrote to Sophie about the difficulty of having a school for the wealthy and one for the poor relatively close to each other. In December 1829, the superiors of the American houses in Lower Louisiana (Grand

Coteau, St. Michael's, and La Fourche) met at St. Michael's. Philippine's report to Sophie delineated her most pressing concerns. Philippine was concerned that the novices at St. Michael's were not getting the training they needed, and the life of the household was entirely disorganized. The spiritual and prayer lives of the community seemed nonexistent. Philippine's letter also included an account of the situation at Grand Coteau. There she found the house to lack any sort of cloister, with people from the town moving through the house without warning. She wrote of fifteen particular concerns, including the observation of cloister, the use of the plan of studies, the need for regular spiritual exercises in community, and the treatment and accommodation of coadjutrix sisters. Philippine also shared her criticism with the community, which was not well received.

After receiving letters from Philippine and Bishop Rosati of Louisiana regarding the education offered at La Fourche and St. Michael's, Sophie realized that the social divisions that were typical in France were not working due to the cultural differences between the two countries. She proposed a solution to Philippine and then entrusted to her the final decision. Sophie responded to Philippine's other queries individually, and generally she encouraged Philippine to show flexibility and latitude for the needs of the American houses, acknowledging that they had different needs than those in Europe.

In 1831, Sophie wrote to Philippine about relinquishing her responsibility as the superior at St. Louis. Philippine, who long had protested her inability to be a leader, was happy to do so. However, Bishop Rosati disagreed, and the decision was reversed. Rosati wrote to Sophie:

> I believe that there is no one among your religious who can gain as much confidence as Mother Duchesne justly enjoys here. All who know her respect

> and venerate her because of her virtues, which joined to age and the experience she has acquired during her long sojourn in this country, make her truly esteemed by all. There are few people I esteem more than this holy religious. She has the true spirit of her vocation, and on many occasions, known only to me...has given the most striking proofs of this....I see from the complaints you heard about her, and which have led you to the proposed change, that she has been misrepresented to you.[1]

Sophie instructed Eugénie Audé to close the house in La Fourche in 1832 due to financial mismanagement and lack of resources. In 1833, Eugénie Audé was named the assistant general of Upper and Lower Louisiana, based on a majority of the votes from American sisters. However, a cholera outbreak had broken her health and heart by this point. At least seven members of the community died, Eugénie ministering to them. By September 1833 she wrote to Sophie asking to return to Europe for a rest. Eugénie's letter arrived in the afternoon of the same day Sophie had written asking her to accept the post of assistant general. Sophie wrote again that evening. The new plan called for Eugénie to make a visit to each house as the assistant general and then return to Europe. This would give Sophie firsthand accounts of the houses which she really depended upon.

When the appointment of Eugénie Audé arrived, Philippine felt freed from the burdens of leadership and again asked to be allowed to serve the Native Americans. Sophie also had to break the news to Philippine that her beloved Ste. Marie d'en Haut had been closed. Sophie asked Philippine for an account of the resources and work the community could do with the Native Americans. In the letter, she spoke sharply of changes that would come to the American houses on the return of Eugénie Audé, and her tone hurt Philippine, who expressed this in her return letter. Sophie's response tried to smooth over the misunderstandings with her old friend.

Eugénie Audé's time in Paris in 1834 brought Sophie up to speed on the events and life of the houses in Louisiana. Sophie used those conversations as the basis for a series of letters written to the Americas between 1834 and 1836, which addressed particular issues that had come to her attention. The first addressed issues of all types, and later letters focused on the needs of the schools. While the religious in Europe knew Sophie personally, few of the seventy-one American sisters in 1834 had ever met Sophie, and her letters seemed abrupt, negative, and overly critical. They read like a list of the American communities' shortcomings. They also came from a culture that differed from their own, and, for some, in a language they did not understand. Thus, the tone and reception of the letters depended on the translation offered. For Sophie's leadership style that depended on personal relationships with individual sisters, this communication with the sisters she would never meet was particularly challenging.

The General Council of 1833 and the struggles of the American houses highlighted the growing pains of the Society in the 1830s. Political tensions, which extended into the communities in Europe, differed dramatically from the troubles of the American houses. There, the hardships emerged more from entering a foreign culture and the lack of both financial and personnel resources. At the same time, the leadership of the sisters was growing stronger, and Sophie was finding the right people to guide growth where she was unable to be present herself.

17
Addressing Scandals

THE YEARS following the general chapter of 1833 included much travel for Sophie, and the new foundations continued. Houses opened in Marseilles in 1834, in Charleville in 1835, and in Brussels in 1836.

The governance structure of the Society was insufficient to handle its growth. During one of her many times of convalescence, Sophie was able to envision and plan to implement a new structure that would enable governance without exhausting her. The stability of the Society seemed assured to Sophie, and she again considered resigning as superior general. She sought support from her spiritual guide, Fr. Favre, who encouraged her to trust in the love and forgiveness of God, not to allow fear to cause her stress and scruples. While he could not help her govern the Society, Favre offered three suggestions to support her in her task: (1) to maintain a rhythm of prayer and reflection that would support her inner spirit and help her keep balanced; (2) to "act as a *general* and not a *foot soldier*"[1]—to maintain the spirit and vision of the Society and delegate details to others; and (3) to listen to the advice of those who cared for her and not focus so much of her attention on penance. He especially encouraged her to remember that her ideal of perfection, to be a perfect model of the Society for the other sisters, was an impossible task. "He challenged her to be humble enough to allow herself to let go of her illusions and live in the reality of her situation, to be led by God, as a little child, into this simple and ordinary path to holiness."[2]

Changing the governance structure of the Society required a new general chapter and approval from Rome. For now, Sophie had to live within the confines of the governance outlined in the 1815 Constitutions. She sought advice from Fr. Rozaven on how the Society of the Sacred Heart could model governance on the Jesuits' structure. He advised that her authority as superior general in the current structure was dissipated by the level of authority given to the assistants general. Their power was too wide-ranging locally so that the local superior seemed to be more authoritative than Sophie herself. He gave the example of Félicité Desmarquest in Rome, who was well known and beloved there while Sophie did not have such a high profile. Sophie's relational style of leadership fostered just this style of relationship between the local superior and her sisters, as the newer leadership developed loving and personal relationships with the novices and sisters they formed and governed.

The original structure intended for the Society included a central novitiate and centralized preparation for final profession, intended to be in Paris, from where the Society would be governed. That initiative was lost with the rapid growth of the Society, for it was impractical to send all novices to Paris, and the houses there were not large enough to handle them. Likewise, the reputation and activities at the Hôtel Biron in Paris made that location impossible for formation. However, a centralized formation would bring all sisters into the same spirit of the Society and prepare them together to go out and serve.

Again hoping for a central novitiate in Paris, the issue of Archbishop de Quélen resurfaced. By this time, he had been a relatively permanent guest at the Petit-Hôtel despite protests of Sophie and others. Eugénie de Gramont even let the archbishop expand his presence into the Hôtel Biron, which also housed the schools. Until 1834, he had been using the Petit-Hôtel for his office and space during the day. In February that year, when Sophie left Paris, Eugénie arranged for an apartment within the Hôtel Biron to be furnished for his use. On hearing this news, Sophie immediately wrote to Eugénie to ask her for greater caution and remind her that the archbishop's presence on the property was causing troubling rumors for the Society. Eugénie, as usual, paid little attention to Sophie's concerns. Beyond the expected impropriety, the presence of the archbishop emphasized a political placement. De Quélen disapproved of the reign of King Louis Philippe and was faithful to the Bourbons. His presence on their campus made it seem as if the Society was aligned with this position, while Sophie urged the religious to remain neutral in the political controversies occurring around them.

In the winter of 1834–35, Sophie, age fifty-six, again found herself ill and spent three months recovering from a fever. During this time, she decided to open a property on rue de Monsieur in Paris, a short distance from the rue de Varenne. This would be temporary, a house for the novitiate and the general administration of the Society—a central mother house. In a circular letter of June 1835, Sophie described the plan for the property.

> This little Society still in its infancy has already made considerable progress...but circumstances have created an obstacle to the fulfilment of the plans which as it were must complete our institute....To achieve this we have decided to have our own residence, which will be the *mother house* or headquarters of the Society. All business will converge there and all plans will emanate from there. The general novici-

> ate [*sic*], the juniorate and the tertianship year for all the French houses will be placed there, as far as this is possible. There will also be the general treasury, the secretariat and the archives of the Society. It will be our usual residence as well as that of the assistants general who will not travel around the houses anymore. In time we will try to ensure that as far as possible two of the assistants general are always there, with the admonitrix and a member of the general council...to help us in our work and form our regular council.[3]

By making this move and requiring the assistants general to live there, Sophie turned the Society in a new direction, with a center away from the rue de Varenne. Sophie wrote in July 1835: "This house [will be] the entire center of the Society and consequently the source from which the true spirit should spring forth and spread, must inspire each and every member who makes up this great family."[4] A new mistress of novices in the centralized novitiate also had the effect of removing that role from Eugénie de Gramont and Félicité Desmarquest, who were often in conflict with one another. Sophie stayed with the novitiate during their first weeks and told the stories of the foundation of the Society including the foundation stories of Amiens, Grenoble, and Poitiers. She spoke of her own role as the foundress of the order. Her presence at the new rue Monsieur house gave time for her to know and be known by the new members. At the same time, she was needed in other houses of the Society.

In her circular letter of January 1835, Sophie wrote,

> My dear daughters in Jesus Christ, there still remains much to be done to reach the perfection of the interior spirit, of mortification, of true and sincere humility,

> required by the sublime vocation to which our Saviour has called us in His Mercy. There is yet a long way to go to reach the truly religious practice of the fundamental virtues, obedience above all.[5]

She noted three elements that were impeding religious from living the high ideal they set out for: criticism of their work and living situations; complaining about those in leadership; and participating in gossip, which divided the communities into competing groups. Sophie asked each sister to look at herself and examine her own conscience.

The next months, April 1836 through January 1837, were spent visiting houses in southern France and Italy. While on her journeys, she decided to confront Archbishop de Quélen, asking him to consider the damage his presence at rue de Varenne was doing to the church and the Society's reputation. She did so in a formal letter to the archbishop on October 14, 1836.

> You are undoubtedly aware...of the shameful and derisive rumors concerning your residence, which are circulating everywhere and which confront and depress me wherever I go. The gutter press has carried these rumors as far as Rome. While the virtue of those concerned is not in question, people are surprised that such rumors can continue to be fueled by failing to remove the cause of these vile calumnies. I myself am spared neither reproaches nor threats. However, that is not what causes me most pain, Monsignor, but the sad certainty of the harm that this situation is doing to your own person....My conscience is alarmed also I must admit in seeing...the reputation, even the very existence of the Society so seriously compromised. I believe

> therefore that I have a duty before God to share my anxieties with you.[6]

The archbishop responded immediately with a letter dismissing her concerns and purporting to move out of the Petit-Hôtel. He compared himself to an Old Testament prophet or an apostle, stating that the one who receives the prophet receives a prophet's reward. Sophie saw that nothing changed, and her response repeated that her concern was for public opinion, and that he was welcome to stay as long as he wished.[7]

The letter to the Society in December 1836 remarked on the heavy load of governance, pointing to the need for restructuring. She spoke of her desire to be personally in touch with each religious, but that the travel and correspondence required were too great a task. She stated that her trip to Rome would be temporary, and she would soon return to the motherhouse on the rue Monsieur.

Arriving in Rome on January 11, 1837, Sophie began the search for a third house that could serve as a novitiate. The Trinità was limited to French residents, and the house at Santa Rufina was not sufficient for their needs. The Villa Lante and the attached Palazzo Lante, also in the Trastevere, became available at a reasonable cost; the Borges family sold it to Sophie by March 1837. The Palazzo needed repairs while the Villa was available for immediate occupation, and the novitiate moved in.

The Trinità had problems that Sophie had to address, too. The superior of the house for the last ten years had excellent relational skills with the nobility in Rome, but Armande de Causans was a poor administrator. In summer 1837, all issues were compounded by an outbreak of cholera. While the Villa Lante and Santa Rufina stayed clear of disease, despite the proximity of the cholera in the Trastevere, seven sisters died at the Trinità. Sophie only heard of it a month later. She was devastated. The need in Rome was profound following the

Image 10. The Villa Lante in Rome, seen from the garden.

cholera outbreak. Sophie encouraged the Trinità to reopen, even without enough teachers, to keep children from losing the education they already had received. At Santa Rufina, children whose families had died were taken into the orphanage.

While Sophie was in Rome, she and Fr. Rozaven could discuss the governance of the Society. He felt that the Jesuit model would be helpful: the superior general held the authority while assistants were only able to assist and advise. All final decisions were made by the superior himself. He advised her to make changes as soon as possible, for her own sake and for the future of the Society, which would struggle to make changes after her death. Louise de Limminghe, still a close advisor to Sophie, shared this vision of a Jesuit governance structure with Rozaven and encouraged Sophie to move forward.

Even in Rome, Sophie continued to hear rumors and innuendo about the situation at the Hôtel Biron in Paris regarding Archbishop de Quélen. She wrote to offer him sole use of the Petit-Hôtel, separating the two houses. The urgency of the situation compelled Sophie to require Eugénie to act. She wrote, "The present situation cannot possibly continue without causing the most serious problems. You can have no idea how much I hear or how much is written to me, I must tell you, from all quarters. Moreover, dear rat,[8] even if these objections did not exist, I think my proposal is the most suitable in all respects. So why should there be any hesitation in accepting it?"[9] Though Eugénie wrote that the archbishop would accept the offer, both he and she continued to delay his removal from the Hôtel Biron. They did not seem to believe or take seriously the public perception that Sophie saw flying around Paris, France, and Rome.

Friends of the Society came to Sophie to express their concern about a second scandal at the rue de Varenne—that it was now the site of high society weddings arranged by Eugénie de Gramont. Eugénie's refusal to listen and obey Sophie's authority was distressing, especially in light of the friendship the two women shared.

Trouble was brewing in Rome, too, where the Society of the Sacred Heart was again a topic of gossip. By 1838, the superior at the Trinità and her assistant were often seen together when going to functions at the Vatican or throughout Rome. The superior was a woman of good manners who got along well with the nobility in Rome, and her assistant was quite capable in running the household, school, and community. However, the lifestyle of the community and the freedom with which the two religious moved around Rome were both causing some scandal. Though religious life in France was more open after the Revolution, there was still the belief in Rome that women religious should maintain papal cloister. Even the pope made it clear that he wished the Religious of the Sacred Heart to live cloister more fully. The tension caused by the criticism directed at the Trinità led the two to consider leaving the Society altogether, taking the Trinità with them. Sophie believed the real issue in Rome was the division among the religious, not the lack of cloister that outsiders witnessed, but she put off addressing the issue until she could reassign the superior after the next general council. The issue was so well-known that Pope Gregory XVI sent a representative to the Trinità to examine the lifestyle there.

Developments in the New World continued. Eugénie Audé was unable to return from Europe due to illness and exhaustion, and the communities felt the lack of leadership. A scandal erupted at St. Michael's, where the superior was blocked from expanding the property by the local community and entered into litigation with support from the local Jesuits. The Jesuits had also given a loan to the Society for the expansion and were asking for the loan to be returned. After receiving the opinions of local sisters, Sophie intervened to reassign the superiors at Grand Coteau and St. Michael's. She also wrote to the Jesuits saying that she was gathering the money to repay them. Sophie wished to open a house in New York, and then to go spend time there herself. In the meantime, there were tensions between the houses at St. Michael's and Grand Coteau, and Sophie begged for them to reconcile. "Do the impossible… to maintain unity between the two houses. Avail of opportunities to help them. And when you can, send some gifts. I would be saddened if the slightest coldness existed between you. The motto of the Society is: One Heart and One Mind, and each one must make the greatest sacrifices to put into practice these two precepts which is so pleasing to the Sacred Heart of Jesus."[10] Sophie also continued to hope that those entering the order in America would be able to have some formation in Europe to imbibe the spirit of the Society together with other sisters in formation.

18

A New Leadership Structure

ALTHOUGH THE issues at the Trinità and rue de Varenne were challenging, bigger problems were emerging.

Preparations for the next council had begun before Sophie left Rome. Laying the groundwork to adapt the governance structure, Fr. Jean Rozaven agreed to draw up rules for a provincial system based on Jesuit practice. Rozaven believed that the current system gave too much of the authority of the superior general to her assistants, and he proposed a provincial system in which their authority would be curtailed. These preparations were kept secret, entrusted only to Rozaven, Sophie, Elizabeth Galitzine, and Louise de Limminghe. Sophie was especially concerned about keeping this information from Eugénie de Gramont and Félicité Desmarquest, for fear they would undermine her plans before the council could begin.

Sophie left Rome for Paris in May 1838. She was not completely well at the time of her departure, and her illness became serious when she arrived in Parma. In the midst of her prolonged recovery, she negotiated the new house in Pignerol, near Turin. Sophie left in late June, taking the baths first for her healing. She then heard of the death of Fr. Favre. Her feelings at the loss were not recorded. Sophie and her companions reached Lyon in the middle of July and Paris at the end of August 1838.

Plans for a general council in Paris or Switzerland were set aside when Sophie got word of a crisis at the Trinità in Rome. The superior and her assistant had left the community during the night of December 7, 1838, to move to a Visitation convent. They said nothing to the community when they left. They both had received permission from the pope and the priest in charge of investigating life at the house. Sophie acted quickly, asking Louise de Limminghe to prevent the news from becoming gossip in Rome, choosing to tell the story that they were called to a council in Paris by Sophie instead. Sophie strongly believed that the two sisters would cause trouble if allowed to remain in Rome, so she asked the pope not to allow them to enter the local Visitation convent. He granted her request, and they chose to enter in Modena instead.

Sophie determined that the situation in Rome needed her personal attention. It also became clear to her that the council would need to take place there. Paris was untenable because of de Quélen's continued presence at the rue de Varenne. Sophie finally called for the council to begin in Rome the first week of June 1839. Unlike previous councils, Sophie did not send out the agenda ahead of time. She only asked that they come discreetly, keeping the destination confidential in order to remain safe in the French political situation.[1] When three sisters responded that they could not make it to the council, including Eugénie de Gramont, Sophie asked them to put in writing that they would agree to all that the council decided. "I have just asked you to send me in writing at least your written agreement to the decrees of the general council. This council will of necessity be decisive for the Society in establishing really solid foundations."[2] She continued: "Storm heaven during that time [of the council], for hell is unleashed against the

Society and is making unprecedented efforts to overthrow it; but if it is dear to the Heart of Jesus, as I dare to hope it is because of the trials he has deigned to send, the gates of hell will not prevail against it. So let us be faithful to be worthy of his protection."[3] All three sisters sent the letter she requested.

The council opened on June 10, 1839, at the Trinità dei Monti. Rozaven presented the changes he thought were necessary to secure the footing of the Society, in line with some of the governance structures of the Jesuits. He presented a total of forty-seven articles, all of which were adopted with little debate. The central changes regarding governance included: the residence of the superior general in Rome; four assistants general to be elected with her and to reside in Rome as well; and provincials who would be assigned to visit houses in a geographical area. The general council or superior general would only visit houses with the provincial present. The superior general would determine the number of provinces in the Society, and provincials would be appointed by the superior general for three-year terms, to be extended to six only rarely. Likewise, local superiors were to have three-year terms. Following the agreement regarding governance structures, on Sunday, June 16, Sophie, accompanied by two sisters and Fr. Rozaven, had an audience with Pope Gregory XVI. While this was not a necessary element of the council, and it did nothing formally, it gave the appearance of approval by the pope.

Changes were made that affected the membership as well. Instead of reciting the Office in choir, sisters were required half an hour of prayer or the Rosary as a more contemplative substitute that would preserve their voices for teaching. Final vows were only to be accepted after the age of thirty and only after at least ten years in the Society. A decree also differentiated the vows said by coadjutrix and choir sisters and gave all sisters the right to wear the profession cross and ring from the time of first vows. With the letter to the whole Society, Sophie enclosed the list of those newly elected to offices and the newly created provinces. The new general councilors did not include Eugénie de Gramont; instead, they elected Elizabeth Galitzine.

The decrees of this council were radical and represented the ideas that Sophie had been considering and working out for years. However, the Society as a whole had not been prepared for such changes. Sophie trusted her leadership style of winning over people through personal relationships, though this would take a long time. At the same time, some of the members were wary of Elizabeth Galitzine and Jean Rozaven's influence on Sophie and the council as a whole.

After the general council ended on July 5, the members met with the pope, and the Jesuit superior general visited Sophie at the Trinità. Both visits seemed to give formal approval to the decisions of the council, though they clearly weren't intended that way. A week later, the members of the council visited the image of Our Lady of Sorrows at the Villa Lante, praying for the future of the congregation. Foreseeing that implementing the council's decrees would entail great challenges, Sophie's letter to the superiors after the council also placed the Society under the protection of Our Lady of Sorrows.[4]

Image 11. Our Lady of Sorrows, Villa Lante, Rome.

19
Opposition

WHILE SOPHIE and Elizabeth Galitzine stayed in Rome to complete the texts and letters following the council, news of the decisions started to make their way around the membership. In Paris, Eugénie de Gramont was not pleased with the decisions of the council. She did not want the center of the Society to move away from France, and she believed the council's decisions showed undue influence by Elizabeth Galitzine, Jean Rozaven, and the Jesuit model of governance. Additionally, the election of Elizabeth Galitzine as a general councilor instead of de Gramont was a blow to the rue de Varenne community. In a letter to the headmistress of the school, Sophie explained some of the prejudices against Eugénie that emerged at the council. Many in the Society were bothered by practices at the Hôtel Biron that emphasized wealth and connection to the nobility.

Sophie also knew that she needed Eugénie's assistance to gain wide acceptance of the council's decisions. She urged Eugénie to withhold her judgment until they could talk about them, and she tried to help her understand them. Sophie's letters even before the council showed that she was trying to prepare Eugénie for needed changes to the governance structures.

She spoke of the need for change after so many years of the previous model of governance, and that these changes were for the good of the Society and each house. Those letters seemed to have had no effect. Eugénie declared that she did not see the changes coming and that she was certain the structures that worked for over twenty years were sufficient for the Society's future. Eugénie shared her criticism with Fr. Joseph Varin, who wrote to Sophie that the changes would obscure the aim of the Society of the Sacred Heart, for the Jesuits had a different goal and aim, and their governance could not be adopted. By this point, however, Sophie no longer trusted Varin to be discreet. Unlike previous councils, she had not indicated to him ahead of the council what she was aiming for, had not invited him, and did not write to him to let him know the outcome afterward. The criticism from Eugénie and Fr. Varin shook Sophie. She asked Louise de Limminghe to pray especially on the Feast of Our Lady of Sorrows and articulated that they must act more slowly and discreetly as they enacted the plans of the council. She also asked Elizabeth Galitzine to compose a response with the help of Fr. Jean Rozaven. This letter would then be distributed to the houses where Varin was expected as well as to the priest himself.

Eugénie continued to send angry letters to Sophie about all the decisions of the council. Eugénie and others wrote to Sophie in the name of the rue de Varenne community arguing against the changes in a way that exposed the strong influence of Archbishop de Quélen. They seemed unaware of the scandal caused by the lifestyle of the community at the Hôtel Biron even though Sophie told Eugénie about it repeatedly. They emphasized the French origins of the Society, pointing out their own Gallican beliefs. These reactions marked one side of a polemic in which Sophie found herself in the middle. De Gramont and the Gallican French sisters were on one side while Galitzine, Rozaven, and de Limminghe were on the other. Sophie wrote to Eulalie de Bouchaud at the noviceship on the rue Monsieur in Paris of her concerns:

> I have received your letter...and I thank you for it, for just now you cannot tell me too much of what you hear from your neighbors [in the rue de Varenne]. Their opposition is definitely supported by Msgr. de Quélen. This then is a disturbance from which we will be delivered by the Heart of Christ. Listen to all but say little and write and tell me everything you find out: that is your task....If this fire spreads it may be necessary for me to go to Paris. Do not say a word about that....Madame de Gramont is taking a path which she could well regret for she can do us harm. This is not her intention but once minds and hearts are divided who can prevent this?[1]

Eugénie de Gramont had been named provincial, and so she was Bouchaud's superior. Sophie reminded Eulalie of this fact and that in all things other than the immediate running of the novitiate, Sophie was in charge.

Sophie tasked Elizabeth Galitzine to write the response to Eugénie's (unsigned) letter from the rue de Varenne. In it, she asserted "that the Society of the Sacred Heart was a universal congregation, not confined to France, and that the decrees of 1839 allowed it to become more truly what it was destined to be: a congregation, modeled on the Jesuits, and serving the universal church."[2] She reiterated that the council had the authority to make these decisions and the membership had the responsibility to live them out.

While Sophie was entrusting Elizabeth with the role to pacify some of the conflict following the council, it was also becoming apparent that Elizabeth did not fully support Sophie's decisions. Elizabeth held strong positions in the Society that favored the Jesuits and Fr. Rozaven, and she moved quickly despite Sophie's more cautious speed. Sophie's direction to slow down, especially in enacting the decisions of the council, was overtly ignored in Elizabeth's letters. Their relationship became further strained as Elizabeth became openly critical of Sophie and disrespectful of her in person. Sophie wrote later that though she was hurt by this, she didn't seek an apology because Elizabeth did not believe she had done anything wrong and so an apology would be meaningless to her.

The situation in France was complex in many ways. The French church was reluctant to accept what was decided in Rome, even in the case of the Society of the Sacred Heart. Yet, as he learned more about Sophie's plans and the governance structure envisioned in the decrees of the council, Fr. Varin became a supporter and saw how it would enable the Society's growth. Other priests who were longtime friends of the Society likewise saw the wisdom in Sophie's vision, which she had been working to enact for many years. At the rue de Varenne, however, the changes were not accepted, and resolution did not come easily. Though there had been many years of trying to rein in the excessive wealth and improper activities of the Hôtel Biron and the influence of both Eugénie de Gramont and Archbishop de Quélen, Eugénie continued her stubborn refusal to submit to Sophie and the desire of the Society. Archbishop de Quélen claimed he would have supported the decrees of 1839 if Eugénie had done so, but the events instead resembled those of Amiens, when Eugénie and others decided to follow Saint-Estève and ignore the authority of Sophie herself. The difference this time is that Eugénie brought the changes to the attention of the French bishops and caused public harm to the Society of the Sacred Heart and to Sophie.

The council of 1839 in effect reformed the Society, and in so doing it opened the areas of past woundedness and division into the public forum. In particular, the division between the French (Gallican) and Roman (Ultramontane) groups in the Society exploded as the Society grew outside of France, reflecting the polarization of Europe as a whole.

Sophie wrote three circular letters that year, attempting to address the council's decrees and their potential benefit to the Society, as well as expressing her distress that sisters would complain to bishops and the pope rather than address their concerns to her. Sophie also adopted a suggestion from Eugénie de Gramont, to try the decrees of the council for a three-year period and then determine at the next council whether they were helpful or not. Eugénie accepted this and wrote that she would promote them in her province of northern France. The relationship between the two women was ever more distant. However, the situation at the rue de Varenne became somewhat more tolerable for Sophie when Archbishop de Quélen passed away on the last day of 1839. Eugénie and others at the Hôtel Biron strove to keep the memory of de Quélen alive by writing a biography and attributing miracles and healings to him after his death.

In her letter to Eugénie announcing her travel to France, Sophie asked her to put in place the 1839 decrees at the rue de Varenne immediately. Sophie's supporters wanted her to act forcefully with Eugénie and remove her from the rue de Varenne, but Sophie was aware that such action would create more problems. Eugénie enjoyed significant support from the nobility in Paris, and she had a following among the communities throughout France. Before leaving Rome in May 1840, Sophie met with Pope Gregory XVI. He reassured her of his support and let her know that a delay in her move to Rome was fine if she needed to remain in Paris to resolve what was going on there. Additionally, he asserted that he would support the important educational apostolate of the Society.

Elizabeth Galitzine, now the provincial of the American houses, prepared for her visit to North America. She first went to Paris, where she had a formal visit with the new bishop, Denis Affre. Unlike his predecessor, this bishop was not in thrall to Eugénie, the rue de Varenne, and their supporters. He expressed agreement with Elizabeth that Eugénie de Gramont should begin to implement the new decrees. Because Affre had at one point written to de Quélen that he should move out of the Petit-Hôtel, Eugénie disliked him and disagreed with him, and she did not keep her views to herself. He in turn disagreed with her way of governance, in that she consulted no counselors and controlled the communication of sisters in the house, especially those who were supportive of Sophie. He also understood that she was mismanaging funds such that other houses were not receiving their due. Archbishop Affre visited the rue de Varenne in September 1840, and he made it known to Eugénie that the priests living in the Petit-Hôtel would be reassigned, and that he would be asserting his authority over her.

Sophie was grateful for the archbishop's decisive action, but it made her visit to Paris even more difficult. She left Italy in August 1840 and arrived in Paris after a six-week journey. In her usual style, she waited to discover the situation before acting. After a couple of weeks at the rue Monsieur, she moved into the rue de Varenne, knowing that while she could not remove Eugénie de Gramont from her post, being present in the house would allow her to reform it more easily.

Throughout the fall of 1840, Sophie kept a busy schedule of responding to letters each morning, holding meetings in the afternoons, and possibly writing more correspondence. By December, she was quite ill, weighed down by the workload, the absence of her secretary, and the weight of the opposition she was facing. She was unable to work until March 1841, aware that during this time Eugénie and much of France remained against her, and Elizabeth Galitzine was spreading the 1839 decrees throughout America.

Sophie's circular letter of June 1841 contained practical elements that needed to be discussed with members of the Society. Kilroy comments,

> By insisting on the sharing of finances and on horizons wider than merely the local community, Sophie was inviting the Society to think of itself as bigger and wider than France, than Europe. She was also reinforcing the idea she had had from the beginning, that the Society was composed of communities served by a central government; it was not a federation, nor were the communities autonomous and independent. All were to be interdependent and in communion with one another. Mobility of personnel and sharing of financial resources as well as a certain freedom from family ties, were essential to the realisation of this model of community.[3]

Sophie's letter also announced new foundations, especially in America.

20

Expansion in America

ELIZABETH GALITZINE made her way through the houses in America. Sophie repeatedly advised her to be gentle and to enact change only slowly, advice that Elizabeth was largely unwilling to follow. Sophie also urged her to act in concert with the advice of others and in accord with the decisions of the council and the writings of the Society, including the Constitutions and other decrees that had been promulgated. However, throughout her two years in America, Elizabeth continually undermined Sophie's authority and leadership.

Elizabeth Galitzine's tour of the American houses gave her the opportunity to share the 1839 documents with her own interpretation. While Sophie understood the decisions of 1839 as a nuanced modification of Jesuit governance, Elizabeth promoted a quick adoption of Jesuit structures. She told the American sisters that after the 1839 decisions were promulgated, the next step would be to adopt the Rule of St. Ignatius. Of course, the council had made no such decision. Sophie also cautioned a slow adoption of the new decrees, with a three-year trial period. She asked that copies of the council decisions be distributed only after a final copy was prepared. Elizabeth handed out unofficial copies and urged quick movement on them. Elizabeth also addressed situations that had long needed attention from the Society's leadership, including the questions about curriculum and teacher preparedness in the New World, and the foundation of new houses. Her manner, Russian ways, and the authoritative role delegated to her by Sophie had a powerful impact on the American sisters. As she visited the different communities, she encouraged them to write to Sophie and ask her to implement the decrees of 1839.[1] Elizabeth's personal contact with each of the American communities and her manner of lobbying for the 1839 council's decisions left those in America with the impression that Sophie was ineffective and Elizabeth Galitzine was more powerful.

Sophie had also given Elizabeth Galitzine the authority to explore new foundations and even begin their establishment. She played a significant role in the foundations in New York, St. Jacques, and Sugar Creek, negotiating with bishops and provincials. Sophie directed her to seek the advice of others, forming a small council of Regis Hamilton and Catherine Thiéfry. On her retreat at Grand Coteau, Galitzine got the idea that all superiors general should make a special vow of allegiance to the pope, like that of the Jesuit superior general. The decisions and governance of the Society of the Sacred Heart would then be overseen by the Society of Jesus, so that the pope would not need to be personally directing the activities of the sisters. Elizabeth herself took two personal vows at the end of the retreat, one to devote her entire life without regard for her own reputation to the Society of the Sacred Heart, and the other to work tirelessly to implement the 1839 decrees as a way to protect it from the destructive forces she thought were at work to harm the Society. While Elizabeth committed herself to the Society of the Sacred Heart, she did so without considering Sophie's position on issues or understanding the complexity of the political divisions Sophie was trying to navigate.

Sophie slowly learned about the damage done by Elizabeth Galitzine in America. The letter-writing campaign she started drew the American sisters into the conflict about the 1839 decrees, a disagreement they knew nothing about. Sophie scolded Elizabeth in a letter, for the "reckless step which you took with the professed members in America, to force us, using the authority of the general council, to adopt your version of the Constitutions! What a door of rebellion you have opened, and above all among the Americans! Fortunately, I received warning in time to prevent the rest of your plan being carried out in Europe. I hastened to warn our provincials here to reject out of hand your proposals in this matter."[2] Elizabeth was afraid that Sophie's caution with Eugénie was reflecting Gallican roots and contrary to the desires of Rome and the Ultramontane party. Sophie was concerned not only about the division within the Society, but also because Elizabeth was promoting changes that were not reflective of the 1839 council and would require changes to the Constitutions. None of the 1839 decrees did so. A new process of approbation would have to be considered if Elizabeth's proposals were taken up. In the process of this, Elizabeth made no secret of her alignment with Father Rozaven and his involvement in the Society's business, which was drawing criticism of him from the Jesuits and bishops. Once again, scandal was brewing in Rome and Paris.

While division in Europe was claiming much of Sophie's attention, the growth of the Society into new mission fields continued. After twenty-eight years on the American frontier, Mother Duchesne's dream of ministering among the Native Americans finally came true. She and her companions went with the Jesuits in 1841 to Sugar Creek, Kansas, where there was a boarding school for indigenous children and a community longing for Catholic leadership. At age seventy-two, Philippine was unable to learn the language of the Potawatomi, and she spent her time praying, mending clothing, and being with the children. Her many hours kneeling in the church deep in prayer earned her the name *Quah-kah-ka-num-ad*, which means "Woman who prays always." Sophie wrote in response to hearing the news:

> What a consolation it was, dear Mother and old daughter of mine, to receive your last letter, undated, but addressed from the Potawatomi village! So at last you have reached the Indian country you have so desired these long years! May Jesus protect you, my dear Philippine, and give you the means to do good there....Have confidence! He [Jesus] will aid you. I keep on worrying about one thing: if you cannot teach your own language to the Indian children, how will you be able to instruct them? Certainly, at your age it will be very difficult for you to learn the Indian tongue.[3]

Very soon after, Sophie made the decision to recall Philippine to St. Charles due to ill health, which Philippine had been hiding from her.

For a few years after that, Philippine refrained from writing to Sophie, believing that the general request sent out to the Society only to write to the superior general with sufficient cause also applied to her. In 1846, communication between the two sisters was restored when Sophie sent Philippine's niece Mother Amélie Jouve to America with a letter from Sophie. "That fortunate niece was received by Mother Duchesne as an angel from heaven. After reading the letter sent to her by our Reverend Mother General, who was her dearest friend, she seemed transported with joy. Tears flowed down her cheeks, and she was speechless with emotion. After a little while she exclaimed: 'So our Mother General still thinks of me, still loves me? She has been so good as to show that love by sending you to visit me?' She was radiant with joy."[4] Philippine responded, clearly moved and healed by the touching message from Sophie and Amelie's presence:

> Your letter, your gifts so exquisitely chosen, have been a life-giving balm, and I have blessed the God of kindness for them....God has blessed me here with a room next to the chapel. I go from one to the other and enjoy my solitude when I can have manual work to do; I have not lacked any for some time. My happiness is to pray for the missions, for the Society, and for you who hold the place of God for me.[5]

21

Rome or Paris?

THE STRESSES of the time, including the apparently irreparable breach in her friendship with Eugénie de Gramont, wore on Sophie, and she again spent much time ill. Several of her long-standing friends and supporters were also ill during these months. Sophie struggled with the workload of the crisis of 1839 and the usual consultation and decision-making that comprised ordinary leadership of the Society's houses. Between 1839 and 1841, nine new foundations were established in Alsace, Italy, France, the United States, and Canada. In 1842, yet seven more new houses were planned in Ireland, England, Italy, Poland, and Algeria. These houses were established while other requests from around the world remained unanswered. Limited finances and personnel restricted the possibilities for expansion. Sophie's decisions were made by choosing places where the houses could thrive and stretch the resources of the Society without destruction. Personnel was a difficult question, as some sisters died young and others were admitted who were not suited to the vocation or the work of the Society.

In April 1842, Sophie and her advisors began to discuss the coming council to take place in July in Lyon. They carefully deliberated who should be invited and how to gain the most support. They chose to foster union through inviting significantly more members than had been present at previous councils, representing all the houses. In her circular letter of June 1842, Sophie asserted the importance of coming together and speaking face-to-face about their disagreements, to come to some sort of resolution for the future of the Society. As Sophie made her way to Lyon for the council, she learned that Archbishop Affre of Paris had written to the bishops of France protesting her decision to move the council outside of Paris without consulting him. Because Eugénie de Gramont had been communicating with him about the decrees of 1839 and the house's opposition to them, he, too, opposed the restructuring of the Society. One of his agendas was to assert his authority as archbishop of Paris over the religious orders in his territory. In writing to the bishops, he also included a copy of Eugénie's notes on the 1839 decrees, as a way to show their "flaws." The archbishop forbade Eugénie to leave Paris to attend the council, and Sophie asked her to challenge him on it, which she refused to do. Sophie could not resolve the divisions in the Society without Eugénie's presence at the council.

The archbishop's letter to Sophie arrived in mid-July, forbidding her to hold a council outside of Paris and requiring her to obey him as her superior. She replied to him outlining her rights as superior general of the Society of the Sacred Heart, including the right to call together a council. Her superior was the cardinal protector in Rome, not any of the particular bishops in places where there were Society houses. The French government had specific rules regarding the communication of bishops, and the clergy in France were held to certain controls by the government. The archbishop's circular letter to the other bishops in France violated those regulations, to which Sophie was not bound. Affre's anger at Sophie was also expressed to the bishop of Lyon, who refused to stand up to

Affre and would not allow the council to carry on in his diocese. Sophie decided to defer the council until there was more clarity, and she wrote a short letter to Affre to again clarify her position. She wrote a lengthier letter to Eugénie letting her know she could have used more support from her in explaining things to the bishop.

Sophie's next act was to write to Pope Gregory XVI for support in her struggle against the archbishop of Paris. Her clear statement of the rights and her understanding of the role of the order's cardinal protector were outlined. She asked him to write a statement that made clear her right to act without the permission of the bishop of Paris, who had never been a superior of the Society of the Sacred Heart. This issue was one manifestation of the tension between the bishops of France and the Roman court, another iteration of the Gallican/Ultramontane conflict. The pope assigned cardinals to investigate the case and the decision was made in favor of Sophie, but their responses arrived too late. The council members, who had already arrived in Lyon when Affre's mandate came, made a retreat and handled some small business items before dispersing and returning home.

The conflict between the French government and Roman authorities continued to be battled out in this confrontation between Sophie and Affre. Eugénie wrote with anger to Sophie, accusing her of harming the Society's presence in France. Archbishop Affre wrote once again to the bishops of France to assert his authority over the Society. As an order recognized by the government of France, French law required all permissions to be sought through the clergy of Paris. He also stated that he accepted the decision of Rome, which placed Sophie and the Society under the authority of the cardinal protector in Rome. This was damaging to the Society in that the French government did not accept any authority from outside France. In the meantime, the Roman cardinals whose instructions to

Sophie regarding the dissemination of the pope's decision had gotten lost in the mail, wrote to her angrily asking why she had not done as demanded. Sophie was stuck in the middle of irreconcilable political and personnel differences.

Meanwhile, Elizabeth Galitzine, who had remained in Lyon, kept her allies Fr. Rozaven and Louise de Limminghe in Rome informed about the situation in France. Rozaven and Galitzine both thought Sophie was done with her role as superior general, too ineffective as a leader and too physically fragile to survive this test. In a letter, Sophie revealed that she thought it was best for her to resign as superior general. "As a result of the position which they have placed me in and the constraints which they consider necessary to provoke me, I can no longer govern the Society. I intend therefore to give in my resignation. It will not be difficult to find a candidate among our mothers who assuredly will govern better than I can. I expect a reply before I leave for Paris."[1] The Roman faction could not understand Sophie's style of leadership and the deliberation she took before acting because they did not grasp the situation and the scandal that quick action would cause. She refused to take their advice or capitulate to their demands.

Seeking assistance in her struggle with Archbishop Affre, Sophie wrote to a long-standing supporter of the Society, Archbishop Césaire Mathieu of Besançon. He responded, reassuring her that he would not abandon her just as she was feeling betrayed. He wrote,

> Allow me in sharing your cross to experience also something of its weight. Simon of Cyrene was glad to have something himself to suffer when he helped our divine Master on the way to Calvary....I can only be hopeful for your congregation. The present storm shows you what success means...and that of the Society is compromising its very existence. But in

> my opinion Providence is teaching you a lesson in humility. For that reason you must accept and carry this cross with great calm, great gentleness, in reverent silence and perfect trust.[2]

When Sophie's niece Julie Dusaussoy died on September 21, Sophie's letter of condolence to her family betrayed her envy that Julie had gone to be with God.

Sophie left Lyon for Paris in early October 1842, and conflict with the French government awaited her. The minister of justice and religion informed the archbishop that the government, which had an agreement with the Society of the Sacred Heart, did not recognize the authority either of Sophie as a superior general or of the cardinal protector in Rome. He asserted that the Society would be dissolved if it did not observe the decrees of 1815, which were what had been agreed to by the king in 1826.

On arrival in Paris in November 1842, Sophie was unsure what to do next. She spent several months of intense stress and negotiation to save the Society. She wrote almost daily to Archbishop Césaire Mathieu, telling him of her doubts and physical frailty. She wrote to Elizabeth Galitzine of the pressure to assert that the 1815 statutes were in full effect, which the French government demanded but which would reverse the decisions of the council of 1839. Doing so would place the center of the Society in Paris once again, and it would be subject to the French government rather than the oversight of Rome. She feared the houses and schools in Paris would be removed from the Society if she did not take such a step. She asked Elizabeth to convey this information to the assistants general of the Society, the provincials, and Fr. Rozaven. Elizabeth, however, took the opposing position, telling Sophie that she should hold tight to the 1839 decrees or risk excommunication in Rome. Sophie's response is filled with reproach for Elizabeth's quick judgment and poorly considered actions. Sophie considered her to be the source of division among the assistants general.

Sophie's help came in the form of the internuncio, Antonio Garibaldi, who worked together with Archbishop Césaire Mathieu to smooth the situation both in Paris and in Rome. Garibaldi explained the situation to the pope's representatives in Rome, articulating Archbishop Affre's role in damaging the Society by bringing its governance to the attention of the French government:

> The government itself, as well as some friends and enemies, holds certain prejudices against this very distinguished congregation, of such benefit in France. In fact, the government considers the Society of the Sacred Heart to be motivated by a spirit quite hostile to the current political order. [It is seen] as a type of congregation similar to the Society of Jesus, or an association over which the Jesuits exercise influence. You...well understand the impact which such prejudices are capable of exercising in France at the present time.[3]

In late November Sophie met with the Archbishop Affre and the minister of justice and religion. The archbishop demanded that she sign two statements, one to reside in Paris and abide by the 1815 documents, and the other to ask the pope to agree that the Constitutions should be in line with the 1815 statutes. Sophie was unable to sign either of those, the first because it would place her immediately beneath Archbishop Affre's control, and the second because it would cause greater division among the Society's membership, alienating the Ultramontane side. She delayed, asking to consult her advisors. Césaire Mathieu continued to send her letters expressing his support. Affre acted like a bully, demanding her allegiance and capitulation without any compromise. He monitored all her movements and correspondence as she stayed at the rue de Varenne. Césaire Mathieu prevented their correspondence from being read by sending it to her through his personal secretary. Affre's actions also alienated the other French bishops, especially those who had Society houses within their territory, by usurping their own authority over the local diocese.

Gradually Sophie determined her course of action. She sought to suppress the decisions of 1839, and so she could sign a statement that she would follow the statutes of 1815, thereby appeasing the government and the archbishop. The French ambassador to the Holy See reassured the French government that Rome would not require Sophie to reside there; Rome was not going to usurp French power.

The general attitude in Rome among those in power was that the council of 1839 was too influenced by Rozaven and the Jesuits in general. Thus, to remove the decisions of that council would be seen as beneficial, a way to show the independence of the Society once again. However, if Sophie were to act to remove these decrees, the division in the Society would be increased. She decided that it would be best if the pope could rescind the decrees, which would keep her out of the process. Her advisors, including Archbishop Mathieu, accepted this arrangement and asked the bishops of the French dioceses that had houses of the Sacred Heart to formally request the pope to suppress the decrees of 1839. Three bishops agreed to draw up a statement and to seek written support from the bishops throughout France, keeping Sophie and her immediate advisors out of the process in order to show that it was initiated wholly by the bishops themselves. A letter addressed to the superior general of the Jesuits acknowledged their role in this difficulty and threatened to bring destruction to them if they were to try to block the move to suppress this decision. The superior general admitted that he was trying to decrease the connections between the two societies and was frustrated by the whole affair.

In the meantime, Sophie received letters from Elizabeth Galitzine and Louise de Limminghe who refused to see the nuances of Sophie's need to compromise in Paris. Sophie could not convince Elizabeth Galitzine that the position of the Society in France required such compromise, and she continued to work against Sophie, this time urging superiors in Europe to petition Sophie to immediately adopt the 1839 governance structures. She also accused Affre of holding Sophie captive in Paris and forcing her to act as he wished. Affre's anger came down on Sophie, who wrote of it to Galitzine, expressing her distrust. "In my grief and in trust I wrote to you as you do with friends, and I did not take time to re-read my letter. To be honest, I was far from suspecting such a swift and serious abuse of my trust on your part."[4] Elizabeth did her best to draw everyone in the Society into her campaign against Sophie, including Sophie's brother Louis. She in turn blamed Eugénie de Gramont.

Sophie spent the time at the rue de Varenne as if in isolation, eating and living separately from the community so as not to give the impression that she favored one side or the other. Eugénie also instructed the sisters not to interact with her. Those who were critical of Sophie and the Gallican side thought that it looked like she was being held captive there, acting only under pressure, which would enable them to question her decisions later. But she did not sign any documents or make any decisions during this time. She repeatedly asked her assistants general to come to Paris to support her, but they repeatedly refused.

In December 1842, Sophie learned that the Roman contingent, composed of Rozaven, Galitzine, and de Limminghe, had decided to split from Sophie and the French houses, developing a separate center in Rome with the remainder of the houses. They had composed their letters to the different superiors and even a letter to Sophie herself explaining their actions. Sophie's anguish grew stronger, and she continued to rely on support from Césaire Mathieu. She waited for the answer from Rome regarding the petition from the French bishops.

Though Sophie kept her distance from the process, the French bishops could not keep the communications entirely confidential. When Elizabeth Galitzine heard of the documents sent to Rome asking for the annulment of the 1839 decrees, she composed her own letters and account to the pope "denouncing the French bishops as well as the leadership in the Society of the Sacred Heart."[5] Her impetuous activity harmed her own position and more or less assured that Sophie's efforts and the request of the twenty-five French bishops would be upheld.

After several meetings ending in early March 1843, the group of cardinals determined that the decrees of 1839 would be annulled, and the Society of the Sacred Heart would live out of the Constitutions that had been approved by Pope Leo XII. Kilroy recounts:

> Mathieu was so excited by the news that on the evening of 3 March he ran round to the Trinità and rang the bell ten times. It was late in the evening, and no one answered. He returned the following morning and announced the news, and then went to Santa Rufina, to do the same and claimed that the ills of the Society were over. Adèle Lehon remarked dryly to him, "but the convalescence will be long and dangerous."[6]

22

A Long Convalescence

THE SUPPRESSION of the 1839 decrees meant an automatic reversion to the Constitutions that were approved in 1826, which resolved the French government's protests. At the same time, the physical inability of Sophie to visit all the houses, due to her own limitations and the extensive growth of the Society, was accounted for by allowing her to appoint delegates, though they were not provincials. In 1843, Sophie was sixty-three years old. Mathieu conveyed the information on the final meeting of the cardinals in Rome, March 4, 1843, to Sophie by letter. Both of them were concerned with how to move forward and how to communicate these decisions to the Society. He assisted her by preparing draft letters for her to use in crafting her communication to the sisters. The division between the Gallican and Ultramontane factions in the Society was not resolved by these decisions, however, and Sophie's leadership continued to struggle with this difficult lack of union. Elizabeth Galitzine, a convert to Catholicism from Russian Orthodoxy, was especially sensitive to any hint of Gallicanism (or anything contrary to Rome). In addition, her role as secretary general had given her power for miscommunication as well as brought antagonism from many members of the

Society. Eugénie de Gramont was also viewed with suspicion, as was the relationship between Sophie and Eugénie, which seemed to indicate weakness in Sophie's handling of difficult situations.

As the tensions with Rome and the French government seemed to be resolving, Sophie began to work on reestablishing her authority and reclaiming the collaborative relationship with the assistants general. All of them had worked actively against her. Sophie described her feelings to Archbishop Mathieu:

> If I could give you the details of their procedures I think you would advise me to maintain a bit of dignity still. They doubted my faith, my allegiance to the Holy See and insinuated this to others, without asking me for a word of explanation....It seems to me that it would be somewhat difficult for me to write to them now, apologize and show them trust. I will certainly take advantage of all the overtures they make to me, to show them good will, understanding and even that the past is forgotten. But to write to them first, I do not think so![1]

Acknowledging the impossibility of the situation, Mathieu challenged her to reach out in kindness, not to apologize for anything as she had no wrongdoing for which to apologize, but to let them know that the trouble would not continue to be a stumbling block in their relationship. He also warned her to keep her distance from Eugénie and the rue de Varenne, though both of them thought it would be impossible to remove Eugénie from the role of superior at this time, regardless of the advice of other voices.

The archbishop of Paris continued to prevent Sophie from acting as she desired. He tried to control her movements and required her to seek permission whenever she wanted to leave the diocese. He also forbade a general council from being convened outside of his diocese. Though she wished to visit the other houses, he forbade her from traveling at all outside the diocese. Archbishop Affre's hostility toward and confinement of Sophie seemed to be exacerbated by his own conflict with Archbishop Mathieu.[2]

In April 1843, Sophie drafted a circular letter to the Society in which she explained the decision to rescind the 1839 decrees. She urged peace and unity among the members of the congregation. Galitzine's response to the circular letter was particularly critical of the residence of Sophie in Paris and the return to the earlier governance structure.

Plans began for the 1845 general council as Elizabeth Galitzine was preparing to visit the houses in America. She left Europe in June 1843, planning to implement the 1839 decrees in those communities. She had left supporters there and hoped they would be a large faction at the 1845 general council. June 1843 also marks a letter from Sophie for the communities in America, asking them to uphold the 1815 Constitutions, which she sent expecting that Elizabeth Galitzine would explain in detail what was meant by this.

Sophie was able to leave Paris when Archbishop Affre's mood changed, and so she made a tour of the houses in Le Mans, Nantes, Tours, Autun, and Besançon. At the last stop she was able to confer with Bishop Mathieu regarding her plans for moving forward. As she visited different houses, she gained a clearer sense of the position of each one regarding the internal conflict and division.

Sophie returned to Paris in September. Though Archbishop Affre again wrote asserting his power over the Society and Sophie, she continued her journey to visit Beauvais, Amiens, and Conflans over the next month. When she returned, she was exhausted and quickly became very ill, an illness lasting two months with convalescence that took a further three. Once again, she found herself bereft of secretarial help, which was relieved by the appointment of Adèle Cahier in 1843. Adèle's meticulous records of the Society remain an excellent source for its history.

In January 1844, Sophie learned of the tragic death of Elizabeth Galitzine in St. Michael's, Louisiana, in December. After traveling extensively throughout the continent, Elizabeth became ill in St. Louis in the middle of winter. She was advised to go to the warmer climate of St. Michael's, without it being known that there was a yellow fever outbreak there. She arrived on November 14, spending some weeks tending to those afflicted. Then on December 1 she became ill herself and died on December 8 in terrible pain. Sophie was saddened to learn that this woman died at forty-three with so much energy and potential still within her. She also learned that Elizabeth had been promoting the 1839 decrees in America under the impression that they would be accepted by the council of 1845 and recognized by the church. Sophie decided to develop a personal relationship with the superiors in America herself, directly leading them through correspondence. She wrote to them personally about the suppression of the 1839 decrees. In her letters, she asked that all copies of those decrees be burned, a drastic measure in order to keep unity among the sisters. She encouraged them to meet and determine how to manage all the houses and ministries in America.

Sophie visited the two English houses in 1844, closing one of them after discovering that there were not the personnel to sustain both. From there she visited the houses in Lille, Jette, and Amiens, and returned to Paris in August. In Rome, the situation continued to be difficult. A public scandal was fed by conflict between the Villa Lante and the Trinità and a perception of Gallicanism. Sophie decided to travel to Rome to attempt to resolve the differences between the two houses and to promote the new governance structures. She also hoped to discuss plans for the next general council with Pope Gregory XVI and the cardinal protector of the Society, Cardinal Lambruschini, both of whom would understand the tension between Rome and Paris.

A fall prevented her from working and from traveling to Rome immediately. She set off from Paris in October with two companions. Along the way, Sophie became ill with a cold and had to recuperate for a month in La Ferrandière. In December, while they were traveling from Avignon to Aix-en-Provence, the weather turned bad, and the coach driver didn't know where to drop the sisters. The walk in the cold made Sophie ill again and they were obliged to delay further. On January 13, they traveled to Marseilles and then boarded a ship for Italy, where they visited the new house at Genoa. They arrived at the Villa Lante on January 23, 1844.

Sophie's presence helped to bring some peace to the household and to the three Roman houses. Though ill throughout the winter months, Sophie received visits from Cardinal Lambruschini. It was clear to both of them that a general council would not be possible in 1845, and it turned out that the council would be delayed until 1851 due to unrest throughout Europe. The 1815 Constitutions continued to guide Sophie's governance. Lambruschini also told Sophie that she must address the issue of the rue de Varenne. Sophie shared her plan with him. She would move in and establish her residence there, thus also claiming local leadership of the house and begin her reform. Both Eugénie de Gramont and Aimée d'Avenas, the headmistress, showed continual disrespect toward Sophie whenever she was present, and they refused all attempts at reform. Sophie wrote to Eugénie from Rome that she must remove Aimée d'Avenas from her office, assigning her instead to write textbooks, which she was talented to do. Sophie also warned Eugénie that more changes were coming.

Sophie and her companions started their return to Paris in June 1845. When they stopped in Turin, Sophie learned that her brother Louis had died on June 21. She spent a day alone and then continued the journey, visiting houses all along the way. Upon arriving in Paris, Sophie began the work of reform at the rue de Varenne immediately with a formal visit to the house. She named a new headmistress. While she did not announce formally that she had taken over as superior of the community, it was clear to them by her presence. Not only did she encounter the refusal of Eugénie to work with her but she also faced the opposition of Archbishop Affre to act in any way according to her needs. Most notably, his assignment of chaplains to the community and school was inappropriate, and though he acknowledged they were not good choices, he would not change them.

Eugénie became mortally ill in the autumn of 1846. Despite their many conflicts, Sophie's love for her old friend showed in her attention to her during these last days. Eugénie died at age fifty-seven on December 19, 1846. Eugénie's funeral was a social event in Paris, planned and carried out by her family with a display of their wealth and connections.

Requests from around the world continued to come to Sophie, for houses to be established in America, throughout Europe, and North Africa. She was always weighing these requests with the personnel and other resources needed for new foundations. She lamented the decrease in novices in the 1830s and 1840s but noted an increase by 1846. The quality of new members was always a concern, and the superiors were constantly asked to refuse those who did not seem to have the spirit of a religious. Deaths, too, marked this time, and many of the first generation of religious were gone. There was a dramatic need for the formation of leadership.

As the Society grew, so did some conflict between the two goals of the Society: to educate the elite and the poor. A frequent concern was the need for quality education, and for the educators to find a proper balance between their teaching and spiritual lives. Financially, the free schools and orphanages needed to find a way to survive without running on debt, and all foundations were expected to pay back any debt they owed.

While Sophie felt the solitude of leadership in her inability to hold a council due to Affre's interference and the division among her counselors, her communication with Philippine once again resumed. Sophie and Philippine, once such great friends, had experienced a rift following Elizabeth Galitzine's visitation of the houses in America. Philippine believed that Elizabeth was promoting Sophie's position regarding the decrees of the 1839 chapter, even while Elizabeth promoted her own interpretation. Additionally, mail service to the American frontier was inconsistent.

By 1847, Sophie wrote to Cardinal Lambruschini that unity was being restored to the Society, though the general council would be needed to make that more obvious. In 1848 and 1849, revolutions began breaking out in Europe, forcing some houses to close which never reopened. The Roman Villa Lante and Santa Rufina communities resided for a time at the Trinità, which the French government had opened for asylum. In Paris, the revolution broke out in 1848, but the rue de Varenne remained in the hands of the Society. Wounded soldiers received help there, and the children of men lost at war were offered education. In June 1848, Archbishop Affre was wounded while he was trying to negotiate peace at the barricades. Before he died of his wounds, he sent apologies to Sophie for the way he had treated her. At this point, Sophie had nearly decided to move out of Paris so that their students could get a proper chaplain to support their spiritual growth. His death allowed that situation to right itself. Additionally, the possibility of a general council once again opened. However, revolutions required additional delays, and Sophie began to seek guidance for the council from Cardinal Lambruschini in 1850.

At the same time, in 1849 to 1850 trouble was brewing again in Amiens. The situation, remarkably similar to that caused by Fr. Saint-Estève decades before, eroded the community and threatened greater division. However, Sophie's experience and confidence led to a completely different response. A priest friend of Sophie's wrote to her in November 1849 expressing concern about a young coadjutrix sister whose entrance he had encouraged. She found the community life in the convent disappointing in that it did not support her or challenge her to a life of prayer and work. Sophie's investigation of the matter uncovered a plot within the community, led by the confessor, Fr. de Brandt, who was spending long hours with a small group of members of the community and preaching publicly in Amiens about a new direction for the Society. He claimed to be entrusted by Sophie with reform.

Sophie Barat herself decided to appear for an unannounced formal visit of the superior general. She arrived on August 2, 1850, with two trusted companions. She discovered that Fr. de Brandt had already written new Constitutions for the Society and named a successor to the current local superior. Sophie removed the current superior and named a replacement, asking her companions to remain there until she arrived. Sophie firmly told Fr. de Brandt of this plan and then left town. He was in no doubt as to her authority as superior, though he expressed his anger before leaving. He would go on to cause further problems with another community and eventually start a group he called the Reformed Society of the Sacred Heart.

23

Fifty Years

THE SOCIETY of the Sacred Heart marked its fiftieth year in 1850. Sophie was seventy years old. Her leadership had developed throughout the decades, and she seemed to trust her style of personal relationships and inclusion for leadership. Though she experienced many setbacks in implementing her vision for the Society, she was convinced to persevere. In October of 1850, she set off for Rome to propose changes to the Constitutions to Pope Pius IX, who had finally returned from exile. She and her companion arrived at the Villa Lante in time for the golden jubilee celebrations planned for November 21. The assistants general had copies made of the image of Our Lady before which the first sisters professed their vows. Sophie spoke on the eve of the celebration, relating the foundational story including Frs. Léonor de Tournély and Joseph Varin.

> But she did not call either of them founders of the Society of the Sacred Heart. Instead, Sophie suggested that while other congregations had founders, who inspired the members to follow them, the Society of the Sacred Heart was different. A loving and compassionate God, revealed in the icon of the

> pierced Heart of Jesus Christ on the Cross at Golgotha, was the founding impulse of the Society of the Sacred Heart. There was the source and origin of the celebration of 21 November 1850. Sophie insisted on this throughout her conference and she cited the words of Christ: "Learn from me for I am gentle and humble of heart." The key to her thought lay in her conviction that in Christ all the energies of God were revealed and available to the members of the Society, who in turn would mirror this vitality in their own lives, in their communities and in their service to the world. That for Sophie was sanctity, that was the cause for celebration.[1]

Following this celebration, Sophie made her case for constitutional changes. Addressing her letter to the cardinal-protector, Lambruschini, Sophie asked for three structural changes in the governance of the Society: the adoption of a system of provinces with provincials appointed to govern them; a new structure for the general council, composed of the assistants general, provincials, and one or two professed members from each province; the right for the superior general to name a temporary successor to govern until the general council could meet and decide the next superior general. After initially refusing her proposal, the pope assigned three cardinals to deliberate. They reached a compromise and announced it by decree on May 28, 1851. Instead of provinces, they required a change to geographic vicariates, with vicars named for life. The vicars would form the governing council of the Society. Her third request was permitted in the form of a vicar general.

Sophie left Rome in June, and she fell ill upon reaching Marseille. After several months of recuperation, she was strong enough to call a council for the fall. The council opened in Lyon on November 13, 1851. The work of the council was divided into commissions for the Constitutions, studies, and formation. The body as a whole debated the proposals brought by the commissions, and decisions were made easily. Sophie's circular letter after the council, the first after years of silence, expressed her deep sorrow for the way the Society's expansive growth had prevented her from developing personal contacts with each member. While she did not address all that had occurred, she articulated that political events had prevented a council from being held sooner. The letter included the warm and loving image that contradicted the wrathful conception of God promoted by Jansenists. Sophie notes in her correspondence that the council was one of unity and consolidation, no longer a source of painful division.

Image 12. Mother House on the Boulevard des Invalides in Paris.

Following this council, Sophie's life became calmer, and her leadership of the Society took on a new pattern. While she remained at the mother house, the vicars made visits to the houses throughout the Society. Sophie's time was filled with even more correspondence to sisters around the world and visits with those who came to her in Paris. "Her health was permanently fragile. Most winters Sophie was confined to her room for two to three months, an annual hibernation which gave her energy for the rest of the year."[2] Adèle Cahier, in service as the general secretary, kept up the communication during those times. The Society continued to open new houses around the world, moving out from North America to South America (Chile) in 1853 and the Antilles (Cuba) in 1858. The list of new foundations between 1846 and 1863 is staggering. Twelve houses opened in France, another twelve in Europe, eighteen in the United States and Canada, three in Chile, and two in Cuba.

While these years marked the growth of the Society, they also marked many deep losses in Sophie's life. Fr. Louis Barat, Sophie's brother and first teacher, died in 1845. Her first mentor to religious life, Fr. Joseph Varin, died in 1850. Her sister, Marie-Louise Dusaussoy, died in September 1852.

Another deep blow came with the death of Philippine Duchesne on November 18, 1852, in St. Charles where the first foundation in the New World had been established. Sophie and Philippine had only communicated by letter since Philippine's departure from France in 1818. Immediately before her death, Sophie sent Mother Anna du Rousier to visit the houses in America on her behalf. Following this visit to North America, Sophie would send Anna to found the first houses in South America. After visiting the houses in the east, Mother du Rousier arrived in St. Charles in November to find Philippine very weak. When Philippine understood that Anna came representing Sophie, she asked for a blessing in Sophie's name. Anna then asked for one in return. Before Anna departed, Philippine exchanged profession crosses with her, blessing her missionary work in South America.

In the 1850s, Sophie made sure that schools in France had the proper documentation. The Loi Falloux was passed in 1850, which allowed members of religious congregations to teach without state-approved training and certification. Yet it was clear that teachers needed training, regardless of the government's requirements. Sophie's attention to the education provided by the Society is exemplified in her concern about the school at Toulouse, articulated in 1855.

> This year we must make amends for the past. To do this successfully we must combine divine ways with practical ones, in caring for the education of the children, in all its dimensions. This includes knowledge in accordance with our plan of studies, handicraft, inculcating the desire, even the love of learning; also the ornamental arts of dancing, drawing and music (*arts d'agrément*), drawing especially. But before everything else they must learn spelling and the art of letter-writing. The other attainments are rare in women but in our time a woman is obliged to write all her life. There are few exceptions to this. So make sure that your teachers instruct the pupils thoroughly in these two subjects. This should start in the 6th class. By teaching these youngsters to spell you will be helping them greatly. Insist on discipline and politeness; make sure the children are trained to have good taste, good manners, with true simplicity. We do not work enough on these essential qualities. Yet these will bind the pupils to us and win their trust, for without this simple and modest way of being, they will not make their way

> in the world. It is the finishing touch to a careful and sound education.[3]

The nineteenth century was tumultuous for the entire world in which Sophie exercised her leadership. While the earliest years of the Society's foundation were marked by the French Revolution's violence and class division, the political turmoil in France and throughout Europe continued. In 1859, the struggle for the unification of Italy began, resulting in the communities being expelled from Milan in January 1860 and Parma in March. While most of the nuns fled, some of them decided to ask for release from their vows. Sophie, in Paris, was canning some fruit that had been blown down by a storm. She used the image to articulate her understanding of the situation:

> The storm is the revolution; the fruits are the religious nourished with the sap of the Society. Some stay attached to the trunk, others fall. Why? Yesterday when you opened the fallen fruit you found a gnawing worm....I see Our Lord with the revolution as a fan in His hand, separating the wheat from the chaff. Father de Tournéley conceived of our Society while the Fathers of the Sacred Heart were fleeing from city to city. We were born in a time of social upheaval; we must learn to live through it safe and sound, and to draw others through it.[4]

Sophie's circular letter of January 15, 1862, pointed to her concerns in this situation: "Children of the Church, we cannot be cold to her sorrows. As she came from the Heart of Jesus on the cross, she must, like her Author, fulfill her mission on the road to Calvary. Our prayers, our humiliations, our generosity will hasten, we may hope, her triumph."[5] In the United States, too, war was at hand. The U.S. Civil War broke out in 1861, and communication with sisters in Louisiana was severed.

In the church, controversial issues emerged that affected Sophie in her role as educator. The Syllabus of Errors, promulgated by Pope Pius IX in 1864, challenged theologians and educators to refrain from using modern scientific studies when examining the faith. Sophie responded with "The Holy See has spoken; let us listen, understand, and obey." She then wrote to Mother Josephine Goetz to get assistance: "Go to priests, consult the Jesuits, and bring me a simple outline of their reflections. We shall pray over this, and I shall make the Society study what we should know and what answers should be given."[6]

24

A Quiet Passing

IN 1862, Sophie asked Josephine Goetz, the mistress of novices, to create a plan for the Society's teacher training. The trust in Josephine Goetz was well-placed, and Sophie knew that she prepared new sisters well for teaching. In 1854, she had appointed her to be the superior of Conflans, and in 1863 she became an assistant general.

At age eighty-four, Sophie became aware of her fading energy, and she called a council for June 1864. The preparations were carried out by Adèle Cahier and the assistants general, focusing on the spiritual life and the educational work of the Society. Three particular issues emerged as fundamental: the preparation of sisters for the work of teaching; the foundation of more houses in the cities rather than the countryside, as requested by parents; and the recruitment of new members in a variety of ways and with different purposes, both choir and coadjutrix sisters. By this time, there were 3,500 members of the Society in eighty-six institutions throughout Europe, North America, and Latin America.

During the council, Sophie also invoked her power to name a vicar general, who would govern if she became too ill or died. This person was Josephine Goetz.

In late 1863, Sophie again succumbed to illness that kept her from other duties and visits. When the new year arrived, she was again able to meet with the community. She expressed her sorrow at the need to be separated from her beloved daughters during her illness, especially as they were mourning the death of one of the others. She said, "The year ended by the Cross, just as it began by the cross; that gives me the confidence that it will be a year of graces, above all of reparation."[1] She then took the occasion of a new year to speak to the community of the virtue of humility and the importance of the humility of the whole Society and of each one to attain God's glory. Over the coming months she worked with Mother Goetz, sharing the worries of the Society with her. Then, again, her health failed. By the beginning of March, Sophie was noticeably frail. That month also, she wrote a circular letter to the Society as a whole.

> Ah how I would speak to you if my strength were in agreement with my feelings! For how can I express to you my gratitude for such filial interest that all the Society has not stopped witnessing to me in these months of testing and absence? I owe to your fervent prayers the improvement of my health, if it improves I will owe you even more. As long as the Lord will consent to conserve for me the remainder of my life which is passing little by little, it will be more than ever consecrated together with the very religious and devout mothers who surround me; their lives greatly relieve me from the painful worries which so often make the government of our Society difficult.[2]

As she so often did, she wrote of her favorite virtue, humility, reminding the sisters of the need to develop it in their lives:

> If I was not afraid of tiring you by always repeating it, I would implore you again, my good Mothers and Daughters, to base all your resolutions on the virtue dear to Jesus, humility. You know that only this catches the attention of our sweet Savior; it forms, maintains, and increases all the others, on this one word ought to be based on the building of Christian and religious perfection. Oh, that we ought to love it! It unites us to the Heart of Jesus, he will recognize only the humble as his true spouses![3]

When she had the energy, which came and went throughout her last months, she kept up her correspondence with sisters throughout the world and with her family. Often her words turned to her coming journey to God. She wrote to her nephew, M. le abbe Dusaussoy, on March 23, 1865: "Do not forget me in your holy sacrifice every day, my dear nephew; I am approaching my end, my age and my feeble strength are approaching signs; help me thus to obtain the mercies of the Lord, I will need it!"[4] On April 29, she wrote to a sister: "This long life seems to be a dream on this side of eternity. Thus let us hurry to satisfy the virtues, graces, and merits, what days remain for us; there will be struggles, no doubt, but they will escape us so quickly that we will not be able to count them."[5]

In the days leading up to her death, Sophie's attention was taken with the children. These days were recorded by Adèle Cahier, who put to paper the stories of others who accompanied Sophie at the end of her life. On May 9, Sophie asked to see the littlest children in groups of twenty, so that she could give special apples to them. A sister who watched the encounter recorded both Sophie's joy at being with the children and their love and admiration for her.

On May 17, Sophie stole out of her room to visit the community. She spoke to them of humility: "Be humble, it is pride that spoils everything, that ties the hands of the superiors, that brings every deficit."[6] Her time and energy did not allow her to see the children that day. On May 21, she spoke with the formation community during recreation, sharing with them different stories and reading letters from the children at Marmoutier.

Sophie began the next day like many others: her time of prayer, a conversation with the infirmarian about the care of someone who was not well, attendance at the Mass, and sorting the mail. At lunchtime, she fell ill and took to her bed. Immediately, Josephine Goetz came to her room and found she was unable to speak. Doctors were called and treated her for a stroke. Sophie's spiritual director arrived and offered her general absolution and the last rites, with the community gathered around. Her counselors arrived over the next two days. Sophie was able to communicate her understanding of the rites and prayers by squeezing Josephine's hand. She was asked to raise her arm in blessing of a sister who was ill, and then to bless the whole Society, which she did with great energy. Over the night into May 24, the community gathered near Sophie, praying the church's prayers for the dying and the litany of the Sacred Heart. Sophie prayed with them, striking her breast during the Agnus Dei, making the sign of the cross, immersing her hand in holy water, and raising the crucifix she held to her lips. Her condition continued to worsen throughout the night, and on the afternoon of the Feast of the Ascension, May 25, her pulse weakened. Cahier recounts,

> At eleven o'clock, exactly, our venerated Mother handed over her soul to God without effort; she became, I am sure, glorified, before the completion of this feast, the triumph of Our Lord in heaven, and

> made true those words she had said the preceding Sunday. Despite the breaking of our hearts, a profound peace upheld us and gave us the assurance that she continued her mission for us there above.[7]

At eighty-five years old, Sophie had served as the superior general of the Society of the Sacred Heart for sixty-two years.

Image 13. Portrait of St. Madeleine Sophie Barat.

25

Unity through the Heart of Jesus

SOPHIE'S LONG life was marked by a world in chaos and a single-minded devotion to share the love of God with those around her. Death often emerged in Sophie's writings and conferences, in which she focused on the work she still had left to do and the need for constant growth in holiness. In a conference on August 14, 1858, she said,

> And do not forget that if we wish our end to be happy we must work unceasingly, with a strong will, to reach that forgetfulness and that detachment from ourselves which must, so to speak, go to excess.... Thus, in growing holy you will make other souls holy, and death will be sweet to you, for it will unite you to the object of your desires: the Heart of Jesus.[1]

At the end of the Constitutions of 1815, Sophie wrote about union in the heart of Jesus, drawing on Jesus's words himself, "That they may be one as Thou, Fr., in Me and I in Thee: that they also may be one in Us: that they may be one as We also are one. I in them, and thou in Me: that they may be made perfect in one."[2] She comments on unity as one of the means of preserving the Society, a conviction based on experiences which multiplied throughout the years. The divisions within the Society did have disastrous consequences, but Sophie's fidelity and strength led the congregation through them to a place of stability by the time of her death. The ideal of union was not just about survival as a congregation but rather a sign of God's presence, an image of God's kingdom here on earth. She wrote, "On this union, therefore, which is the work of grace, rests all the hopes of this little Society; by this union of minds and hearts it will maintain and strengthen itself, and spread more and more for the greater glory of God, for the propagation of the worship of the Sacred Heart and for the sanctification of souls."[3]

Union of the members of the Society with one another emerges when each one contemplates and studies the heart of Jesus, learning from Jesus to love as he loves—personally, abundantly, and tenderly. Sophie exemplified this tender love for her sisters, even those who caused her great trouble. Her ability to bridge the many divisions in the Society and in the world around her contributed to the rebuilding of France after the Revolution. It fostered a strong unity in the Religious of the Sacred Heart around their charism to discover and reveal the heart of Jesus in the world. The congregation, well-established after her sixty-five years of leadership, continues to work toward unity and reconciliation of differences today through contemplation of the heart of Jesus and tender care of relationships.

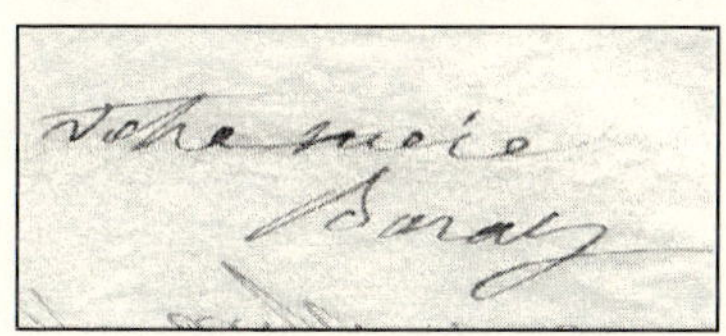

Image 14. Signature of Sophie Barat from one of her fourteen thousand letters, "Votre mère, Barat" ("Your mother, Barat").

Notes

FOREWORD

1. Phil Kilroy, *Madeleine Sophie Barat: A Life* (New York: Paulist Press, 2000).

CHAPTER 1

1. "Notes sur notre fondatrice et les commencements de la Société. Premiers jours de la Société du Sacré Coeur de Jésus" (General Archives, Society of the Sacred Heart, Rome, A-II., 1-a, Box 1); trans. Phil Kilroy, in *Madeleine Sophie Barat: A Life* (New York: Paulist Press, 2000), 15.

2. Margaret Ward, *Life of Saint Madeleine Sophie: Foundress of the Society of the Sacred Heart of Jesus, 1779–1865* (Roehampton: Convent of the Sacred Heart, 1925), 18.

CHAPTER 2

1. Adèle Cahier, *Vie de la Vénérable Mère Barat: Fondatrice et première supérieure générale de la Société du Sacré-Coeur de Jésus*, 2 vols. (Paris: E. de Soye et fils, imprimeurs 1884), 1:31, citing a community gathering in 1864 in which Sophie told this story. Trans. Margaret Williams in *St. Madeleine Sophie: Her Life and Letters* (New York: Herder and Herder, 1965), 47–48.

2. Pauline Perdrau, *Les Loisirs de l'Abbaye, Souvenirs inédits de Pauline Perdrau sur la vie de notre sainte mère* (Rome, 1934), 1:422–24;

trans. Phil Kilroy in *Madeleine Sophie Barat: A Life* (New York: Paulist Press, 2000), 39. Emphasis original.

CHAPTER 3

1. Phil Kilroy, *Madeleine Sophie Barat: A Life* (New York: Paulist Press, 2000), 43.

2. Sophie Barat to Philippine Duchesne, Amiens, February 3, 1806. *Letters of Saint Madeline* [*sic*] *Sophie Barat to Our Religious (Translated from the French)* (Internal publication of the Society of the Sacred Heart), 1:8–9.

CHAPTER 4

1. Although the council made this decision, the name of the congregation would not be settled for many years.

2. Sophie Barat to Philippine Duchesne, Poitiers, August 1, 1806. *Letters of Saint Madeline* [*sic*] *Sophie Barat to Our Religious (Translated from the French)* (Internal publication of the Society of the Sacred Heart), 1.11.

CHAPTER 5

1. "Manuscrit de la Mere Thérèse Maillucheau," 158–74; trans. Phil Kilroy in *Madeleine Sophie Barat: A Life* (New York: Paulist Press, 2000), 68.

2. Kilroy, *Madeleine Sophie Barat*, 77: "ostensibly for political activity in Amiens and for interfering with the affairs of the local diocese."

CHAPTER 6

1. Sophie Barat to Saint-Estève, Paris, September 11, 1813, "Amiens Affaires, Lettre No. 2,"; trans. Phil Kilroy in *Madeleine Sophie Barat: A Life* (New York: Paulist Press, 2000), 80. Emphasis original.

2. Kilroy, *Madeleine Sophie Barat*, 90.

3. Response to Mr. Lampert, Paris, December 1, 1815, "Amiens Affaires 1814–1816"; trans. Kilroy in *Madeleine Sophie Barat*, 98.

CHAPTER 7

1. Society of the Sacred Heart, Constitutions (1815), 4. The original Constitutions of 1815 are used by all RSCJ today alongside the new Constitutions that were composed following the Second Vatican Council.

2. Constitutions (1815), 5.

3. Constitutions (1815), 67.

4. Constitutions (1815), 201.

5. Constitutions (1815), 329.

6. Sophie Barat to her sisters, Paris, December 17, 1815, "Affaires Amiens no. 44"; trans. Phil Kilroy, in *Madeleine Sophie Barat: A Life* (New York: Paulist Press, 2000), 97.

CHAPTER 8

1. Sophie Barat to Emilie Giraud, Letter 38, Amiens, October 5, 1814; trans. Phil Kilroy in *Madeleine Sophie Barat: A Life* (New York: Paulist Press, 2000), 102.

2. Kilroy, *Madeleine Sophie Barat*, 104–5.

3. Kilroy, *Madeleine Sophie Barat*, 107.

4. Kilroy, *Madeleine Sophie Barat*, 109.

CHAPTER 9

1. Translated by Louise Callan in *Philippine Duchesne: Frontier Missionary of the Sacred Heart 1769–1852* (Westminster, MD: Newman Press, 1957), 232.

CHAPTER 10

1. Phil Kilroy, *Madeleine Sophie Barat: A Life* (New York: Paulist Press, 2000), 141–42.

2. Sophie Barat to Thérèse Maillucheau, Chambéry, September 3, 1819; trans. Margaret Williams in *St. Madeleine Sophie: Her Life and Letters* (New York: Herder and Herder, 1965), 235.

CHAPTER 11

1. Sophie Barat to Alida Dumazeaud, Letter 79, Paris, November 29, 1852; trans. Phil Kilroy in *Madeleine Sophie Barat: A Life* (New York: Paulist Press, 2000), 145.

2. Kilroy, *Madeleine Sophie Barat*, 147.

3. According to Kilroy, this is found in the memoirs of Marie de Flavigny, *Mémoires de la Comtesse d'Agoult*. See *Madeleine Sophie Barat*, 152.

4. Kilroy, *Madeleine Sophie Barat*, 158.

CHAPTER 12

1. Joseph-Marie Favre to Sophie Barat, December 15, 1824, printed in François Bouchage, *Le serviteur de Dieu, Joseph-Marie Favre, maître et modèle des ouvriers apostoliques, 1791–1838* (Paris, 1901), 513–14; trans. Phil Kilroy in *Madeleine Sophie Barat: A Life* (New York: Paulist Press, 2000), 164. Emphasis original.

2. Joseph-Marie Favre to Sophie Barat, Chambéry, August 25,1832. Bouchage, *Le serviteur de Dieu*, 517; trans. Kilroy in *Madeleine Sophie Barat*, 214.

CHAPTER 13

1. Circular letter, August 11, 1826. Unattributed and unpublished translation provided by the Society of the Sacred Heart National Archives, United States-Canada.

2. Phil Kilroy, *Madeleine* [*sic*] *Sophie Barat: A Life* (New York: Paulist Press, 2000), 175.

3. Rozaven to Naudet, May 9, 1821; trans. Kilroy in *Madeleine Sophie Barat*, 177–78.

4. Sophie Barat to Mademoiselle Galitzin, Paris, October 2, 1825. *Letters of Saint Madeline* [*sic*] *Sophie Barat to Our Religious (Translated from the French)* (Internal publication of the Society of the Sacred Heart), 2.61.

5. Sophie Barat to Mademoiselle Galitzine, December 15, 1826. *Letters*, 2:94–95.

6. Sophie Barat, *Conferences* 1:16 (June 2, 1827); trans. Margaret Williams in *St. Madeleine Sophie: Her Life and Letters* (New York: Herder and Herder, 1965), 246–47.

CHAPTER 14

1. Paris, December 9, 1827, trans. Margaret Williams in *St. Madeleine Sophie: Her Life and Letters* (New York: Herder and Herder, 1965), 234.

2. Sophie Barat to Eugénie Audé, Letter 29, Paris, February 28, 1826; trans. Phil Kilroy in *Madeleine Sophie Barat: A Life* (New York: Paulist Press, 2000), 189.

3. Sophie Barat to Sister de Rozeville, October 27, 1828, *Letters of Saint Madeline* [*sic*] *Sophie Barat to Our Religious (Translated from the French)* (Internal publication of the Society of the Sacred Heart), 2:136.

4. Kilroy, *Madeleine Sophie Barat*, 191.

5. Sophie Barat to Philippine Duchesne, Letter 254, Paris, June 26, 1829; trans. Kilroy, in *Madeleine Sophie Barat*, 195.

CHAPTER 15

1. Sophie Barat to Emilie Giraud, Rome, March 4, 1837, Lettres Sup, 1:98; trans. Margaret Williams in *St. Madeleine Sophie: Her Life and Letters* (New York: Herder and Herder, 1965), 331.

2. Sophie Barat to Eugénie de Gramont, Letter 282, September 6, 1831; trans. Phil Kilroy in *Madeleine Sophie Barat: A Life* (New York: Paulist Press, 2000), 207.

CHAPTER 16

1. Joseph Rosati to Sophie Barat, Letter 137, St. Louis, February 1, 1832 (Society of the Sacred Heart National Archives, USA. Callan Collection, 13, 3, 2–11); trans. Phil Kilroy in *Madeleine Sophie Barat: A Life* (New York: Paulist Press, 2000), 231.

CHAPTER 17

1. Phil Kilroy, *Madeleine Sophie Barat: A Life* (New York: Paulist Press, 2000), 239.

2. Kilroy, *Madeleine Sophie Barat,* 240.

3. Circular letter, 1, Paris, June 4, 1835, 54–55; trans. Kilroy in *Madeleine Sophie Barat,* 249.

4. Circular letter, 1, Paris, June 28, 1835, 61; trans. Kilroy in *Madeleine Sophie Barat,* 249.

5. Circular letter, Lyons, January 1835. Unattributed and unpublished translation provided by the Society of the Sacred Heart National Archives, United States-Canada.

6. Sophie Barat to Archbishop de Quélen, Letter 1, Chambéry, October 18, 1836 (Archives de l'Archevêché de Paris, Papiers de Quélen, 1 D 4 10, No. 19 a); trans. Kilroy in *Madeleine Sophie Barat,* 253–54.

7. Kilroy, *Madeleine Sophie Barat,* 254.

8. This was apparently an endearment.

9. Sophie Barat to Eugénie de Gramont, Letter 634, Rome, January 18, 1838; trans. Kilroy in *Madeleine Sophie Barat,* 263.

10. Sophie Barat to Aloysia Hardey, Letter 5, Rome, December 30, 1837; trans. Kilroy in *Madeleine Sophie Barat,* 262.

CHAPTER 18

1. *Circular Letters of the Venerable Mother Madeleine Sophie Barat: Letters for Superiors, Councilors and Treasurers* (Roehampton: House of the Sacred Heart, 1904), 2:72–75.

2. Sophie Barat to Eugénie de Gramont, Rome, May 26, 1839 (Société du Sacré-Coeur, Archives Françaises, Poitiers, A-4, Constitutions, Conseil de 1839); trans. Phil Kilroy in *Madeleine Sophie Barat: A Life* (New York: Paulist Press, 2000), 284.

3. *Circular Letters,* 2:77.

4. Rome, 13 July 1839, *Circular Letters,* 2:46.

CHAPTER 19

1. Sophie Barat to Eulalie de Bouchaud, Letter 45, Rome, October 5, 1839; trans. Phil Kilroy in *Madeleine Sophie Barat: A Life* (New York: Paulist Press, 2000), 295–96.

2. General Archives, Society of the Sacred Heart, Rome, C-I., c-3, Box 3, 1839; trans. Kilroy in *Madeleine Sophie Barat*, 296.

3. Kilroy, *Madeleine Sophie Barat*, 330.

CHAPTER 20

1. Phil Kilroy, *Madeleine Sophie Barat: A Life* (New York: Paulist Press, 2000), 334.

2. Sophie Barat to Elizabeth Galitzine, Letter 173, Rome, April 25, 1842; trans. Kilroy in *Madeleine Sophie Barat*, 337.

3. Sophie Barat to Philippine Duchesne, August 23, 1841; trans. Louise Callan in *Philippine Duchesne: Frontier Missionary of the Sacred Heart 1769–1852* (Westminster, MD: Newman Press, 1957), 644–45.

4. *Notes* by Mother Jouve, trans. Callan in *Philippine Duchesne*, 687.

5. Philippine Duchesne to Sophie Barat, September 10, 1847; trans. Frances Gimber, *Philippine Duchesne: Pioneer on the American Frontier (1769–1852)* (Society of the Sacred Heart, 2019), 2:598–600.

CHAPTER 21

1. Sophie Barat to Cardinal Pedicini, Lyon, September 22, 1842 (General Archives, Society of the Sacred Heart, Rome, C-I., c-3, Box 2, 1839); trans. Phil Kilroy, in *Madeleine Sophie Barat: A Life* (New York: Paulist Press, 2000), 351.

2. Césaire Mathieu to Sophie Barat, Letter 2, Paris, October 8, 1842; trans. Kilroy, in *Madeleine Sophie Barat*, 353.

3. Antonio Garibaldi to Lambruschini, Paris, October 15, 1842 (Archivio Segreto Vaticano, Fonds Segretario di Stato Esteri, Busa 616, Rubrica 283, Fascicolo 1, no. 1738); trans. Kilroy in *Madeleine Sophie Barat*, 354.

4. Sophie Barat to Elizabeth Galitzine, Letter 192, Paris, December 6, 1842; trans. Kilroy, in *Madeleine Sophie Barat*, 365.

5. "Représentation faites sur le Mémoire adressée sa Sainteté sur la situation actuelle de la Société des Dames du Sacré-Coeur" (Affaires concernant la Société de 1839 à 42. no. 2, ff. 12–25.); trans. Kilroy, in *Madeleine Sophie Barat,* 371.

6. Kilroy, *Madeleine Sophie Barat,* 371–72.

CHAPTER 22

1. Sophie Barat to Césaire Mathieu, Letter 41, Paris, February 15, 1843; trans. Phil Kilroy, in *Madeleine Sophie Barat: A Life* (New York: Paulist Press, 2000), 375.

2. Kilroy, *Madeleine Sophie Barat,* 380.

CHAPTER 23

1. Phil Kilroy, *Madeleine Sophie Barat: A Life* (New York: Paulist Press, 2000), 412.

2. Kilroy, *Madeleine Sophie Barat,* 417.

3. Sophie Barat to Pauline Pellison de Valencise, Letter 5, Paris, October 26, 1855; trans. Kilroy, in *Madeleine Sophie Barat,* 426–27.

4. Pauline Perdrau, *Les Loisirs de l'Abbaye, Souvenirs inédits de Pauline Perdrau sur la vie de notre sainte mère* (Rome, 1934), 1:201; trans. Margaret Williams, *St. Madeleine Sophie: Her Life and Letters* (New York: Herder and Herder, 1965), 412.

5. Circular letter, January 15, 1862; trans. Williams, *St. Madeleine Sophie,* 548.

6. Perdrau, *Les Loisirs de l'Abbaye,* 2:309; trans. Williams, *St. Madeleine Sophie,* 551.

CHAPTER 24

1. Adèle Cahier, *Vie de la Vénérable Mère Barat: Fondatrice et première supérieure générale de la Société du Sacré-Coeur de Jésus* (E. de Soye et fils, imprimeurs: Paris, 1884), 2:638. Author's translation.

2. Circular letter, March 10, 1864. Unattributed and unpublished translation provided by the Society of the Sacred Heart National Archives, United States-Canada.

3. Circular letter, March 10, 1865. Unattributed and unpublished translation provided by the Society of the Sacred Heart National Archives, United States-Canada.

4. Cahier, *Vie de la Vénérable Mère Barat*, 2:644. Author's translation.

5. Cahier, *Vie de la Vénérable Mère Barat*, 2:645. Author's translation.

6. Cahier, *Vie de la Vénérable Mère Barat*, 2:648. Author's translation.

7. Cahier, *Vie de la Vénérable Mère Barat*, 2:653. Author's translation. Cahier records this scene as an account given to her by the Mother Vicar General, 2:650–3.

CHAPTER 25

1. Sophie Barat, *Conférences de la vénérable Mère Madeleine Sophie Barat fondatrice de la Société du Sacré-Coeur de Jésus* (Convent of the Sacred Heart: Roehampton, 1900), 2:369. Author's translation.

2. Constitutions (1815), 329.

3. Constitutions (1815), 323.

Praise for *By the Waters of Paradise*

"*By the Waters of Paradise* is both an intimate memoir and a history of racism, religion, and politics, and Kinberg reveals her aunt's story with sensitivity. She discovers the jagged intersections of Jewish and Black history in the United States, where white supremacy, Christian nationalism, and capitalism delimited each group's opportunities in turn—and sometimes in startlingly entangled ways."

—Lila Corwin Berman, professor of history and of Hebrew and Judaic studies, New York University

"The question of who we are always invokes questions of whom we come from, when and where we live, and how we make choices within circumstances we don't choose. Through the life of an independent-minded aunt she never met, Clare Kinberg explores generations of Jewish, Black, and lesbian life. In her deft hands, one family's history resounds as a quintessential story of the American century."

—Robin Bernstein, author of *Freeman's Challenge*

"In seeking to bring the hidden story of her deceased Aunt Rose to light, Clare Kinberg illuminates her family's—and the nation's—history and, along the way, sheds a great deal of light on our present moment. With a keen eye on the roles that race, sexuality, and religion played in the story of Aunt Rose's life, Kinberg compellingly weaves together personal, local, national, and global histories while offering profound meditations upon the complicated nature of family and identity. *By the Waters of Paradise* blends archival research, family lore, and imaginative speculation together in the richest possible way."

—Robert Erlewine, director, Eastern Michigan University Center for Jewish Studies

"*By the Waters of Paradise* is truly a beautiful, poignant, and well-researched book. The segregation and lesbian narratives weave and undergird both this Jewish family story and the niece-aunt connection."
—Shonda Buchanan, author of *Black Indian* (Wayne State University Press) and *The Lost Songs of Nina Simone*

"Why did Clare Kinberg, who formed an interracial family of her own, not know about her father's sister, her Aunt Rose, who did the same thing fifty years earlier? In this moving memoir, Kinberg solves that mystery as she explores African American and Jewish history to discover the Jewish roots of her strong moral opposition to anti-Black racism—an opposition that she found lacking in her father's house. *By the Waters of Paradise* is an illuminating and nuanced account that brings the reader to a deeper understanding of identity, race, religion, gender, and power in the lives of Black and Jewish Americans."
—Rebecca Alpert, professor emeritus of religion, Temple University

"Quietly, Clare Kinberg takes us on a profound revelation of the pervasive codes of racism and usurpations that shaped her birth family, and how deeply American it all is. A blurred image of her Aunt Rose, the shunned daughter of a loving Jewish family in the 1940s, leads Kinberg on a journey into the thick layerings of displacement—familial and national—that American racism demanded and still does. In answer, we find vibrant Black communities of memory, new familial promises, a more complex national self. It is a personal search into a family exile that is profoundly national."
—Joan Nestle, author of *A Restricted Country* and *A Fragile Union*